Philosophical Essays

TEODROS KIROS

PHILOSOPHICAL ESSAYS

The Red Sea Press, Inc.
Publishers & Distributors of Third World Books

P. O. Box 1892
Trenton, NJ 08607

RSP

P. O. Box 48
Asmara, ERITREA

The Red Sea Press, Inc.
Publishers & Distributors of Third World Books

| P. O. Box 1892 |  | P. O. Box 48 |
| Trenton, NJ 08607 | | Asmara, ERITREA |

Copyright © 2011 Teodros Kiros
First Printing 2011

Book and cover design: Saverance Publishing Services

Library of Congress Cataloging-in-Publication Data

Kiros, Teodros, 1951-
  Philosophical essays / Teodros Kiros.
      p. cm.
  Includes bibliographical references and index.
    ISBN 1-56902-337-9 (hard cover) -- ISBN 1-56902-338-7
(pbk.) 1. Democracy--Philosophy. I. Title.
JC423.K527 2011
321.801--dc22

I dedicate this book to my deceased parents, Mr. Kiros Ghezhegn and Mrs. Alemsehai Mitku; my sister Arsema Mesfin, who devotedly established all my contacts in Ethiopia; and my brother Solomon Kiros, who died in the prime of his life.

CONTENTS

FOREWORD
BY GEORGE KATSIAFICAS

Only a fool or a philosopher would dare question whether or not the USA, "the world's most free society," is a democracy. Yet this is precisely the question that must be asked today, unless we choose to ignore much of recent history. No less than the collapse of twentieth century communism, the continuing wars of mass destruction in Iraq and Afghanistan waged by the world's greatest democracy signals a crisis of civilization—and of the basic vocabulary with which we discuss it. A contemporary swath of devastation from Palestine to Pakistan, perpetrated in the name of freedom, is only the latest episode in a long history of American genocide that stretches from Native America to the Philippines, Korea to Vietnam, and Iraq to Afghanistan. Is wanton war therefore an essential part of democracy?

The dialectical character of the US—its simultaneous appearance as a free society and humanity's most murderous incarnation—presents us with an intractable contradiction. The crown of creation of European thought and action, the United States of America is much more than that, embodying humanity's great experiment in mixing together all the world's ethnicities and cultures in a beautiful country whose bountiful resources could easily yield plenty for all. American democracy means dissident opinions, no matter how unpopular, do not normally result in imprisonment or death. Individuals are free to choose to their own professions and places of residence, and citizens enjoy a wide range of liberties denied to many of the world's people.

As an American born in Texas of Greek ancestry who grew up on US army bases in Germany and Taiwan and in the inner cities of Baltimore, New York and Boston, I have witnessed in my life-time the global failure of this "democratic" political system to fulfill its promises of government "of the people, by the people, and for the people." Today's descent of the US, by which I understand its decreasing liberties, increasing cultural barbarism, dumping down of its people, collapse of its infrastructure, and intensification of its wars against the wretched of the earth, calls into question the basic meaning of what constitutes democracy.

Although imposed at the point of the bayonet today in Iraq, modern Western democracy emanates from a philosophical tradition whose unfolding logic led precisely toward more freedom, as Kiros convincingly portrays in the following pages. From Plato and Aristotle through Rousseau and Marx, the logical progression of European thought pointed toward greater liberty, to a radical conception of democracy in which the people's capacity for self-government was central—not the unlimited powers of militarized nation-states. In our world, at least 30,000 children die daily of unnecessary causes like inadequate food and polluted water, while the horror of corporate capitalism claims to epitomize freedom, just as the monstrous edifice constructed by twentieth century communism claimed roots in Karl Marx's vision. It matters little that Marx envisioned the abolition of the state through the activation of grassroots democracy, a higher level of the participatory democracy, which emerged first in ancient Greece.

While Greece is commonly understood as the birthplace of democracy, recent evidence has uncovered republican forms of government in ancient Sumeria and among merchants of India. What Greece appears to have contributed to humanity's unfolding democracy project was the participation of all citizens as equals, a notion radically refreshing when we recall that offices in democratic city-states were sometimes determined by lottery to assure to everyone an equal opportunity of the privilege of serving his fellows. Yes, women were denied the franchise in ancient Greece, as were all non-citizens, including slaves who constituted as much as one-third of ancient Athens. Simultaneously, male citizens enjoyed unrivaled equality of opportunity to speak openly and participate in political decisions. Kiros's very name ties him to ancient Greece and stands as a living example of the ties that for centuries bound together the freedom loving peoples of northeast Africa and their Greek-speaking neighbors to the north. Against both the Persian behemoth and the subsequent Roman conquest, the free Greeks and Nubians shared common cause.

In these brief essays, originally written by Teodros Kiros to explain to Ethiopian readers classical Western political philosophy, the author departs from precisely such an embedded understanding of world affairs and posits "pure democracy" as an alternative to the bankrupt regimes that today govern in the name of their people. Since he was born an Ethiopian and remains true in his heart to his homeland, Kiros pauses at several key points in his exposition of the classical tradition to apply its concepts to the Ethiopian context. While largely ignored in the West, the Ethiopian regime, like its patron in Washington, rules in the name of the people while perpetrating war and policies in the interests of the indigenous elite—not the masses of its people. In 2005, after fraudulent elections reminiscent of the Bush family's theft of Florida in 2000, unarmed students went into the streets of Addis Ababa—and police massacred at least 40 teenagers. Before the bloodletting stopped, more than 193 persons lay dead and 20,000 had been arrested—all in the name of democracy. The sacred grounds of Haile Salassie University, once the palace of the last of the long line of Ethiopian emperors, ran red with the blood of African youth. When "democratically" selected leaders ordered their security forces to turn their weapons on the flower of their own land, they thereby forfeited any right to claim the reins of government—except for their "democratic mandate. If this bloodshed had occurred in Iran, the American media would still be covering it, but because it transpired in a US ally in an all but forgotten part of the world, little notice was taken at the time, and none in its aftermath.

Like the majority of Ethiopian citizens, Kiros was powerless to do anything about the massacre perpetrated by the Meles regime. As a philosopher, he employs the weapon of criticism to struggle against dictatorship. By naming "pure democracy" as his goal, Kiros makes apparent the inadequacy of Ethiopian regime, and in so doing, he unwittingly lays bare the hollow core of the entire model of Western democracy. Gleaned from his columns in the *Ethiopian Reporter* over the last nine years, Kiros' essays summarize the essential thoughts of those who produced Western democracy and continue that tradition through an immanent development of the concept of democracy. In so doing, his insights are universally valid. Nowhere today—with the possible exception of places like Venezuela, Ecuador, and Bolivia—does democracy have anything to do with rule by the people. Participatory democracy was a dream of the movements of the 1960s, whose meteoric rise and decline left untouched the purity of that vision.

I first became acquainted with Teodros Kiros as I overheard him mention Fanon in a conversation across a sauna. Incredulous that we shared a common interest in radical thought, we soon became extraordinary friends. As we enjoyed long conversations into the morning hours and got to know the intimate details of each other's lives, we developed a mutual capacity to push each other in directions that we needed to explore. I encouraged him to ground his thinking in social movements, and he sought to elevate my theorizing movements on a more abstract plane. We co-edited a book on multiculturalism and labored collaboratively editing a peer-reviewed journal. In preparation for a conference in Addis Ababa in 1996, I perused the work of fourteenth century philosopher Ibn Khaldun and wrote an essay comparing his philosophy of history with that of G.W. F. Hegel.

In this period, Teodros was in the midst of developing his elucidation of Ethiopian philosopher Zara Yacoub, whose philosophy "of the heart" led Kiros to ground his thinking in the ancient Egyptian notion of Mat. (Unlike the modern assumption that thinking is rooted in the brain, the Egyptians understood it as emanating from the heart.) In a more modern context, the sensuous thought of Zara Yacoub has many parallels to my teacher, Herbert Marcuse, whose thinking exploded the Western mind/body split that has corrupted much of European thought since Descartes.

Remaining true to his Ethiopian roots, Teodros Kiros found few American academics willing to engage themselves with the African oral tradition—let alone to recognize Zara Yacoub as worthy of the stature accorded him in Kiros's writings. Rather, Kiros found himself—a scholar rooted in classical European philosophy who was at the cutting edge of writing a history of African philosophy—continually asked to teach courses on African-American history and race relations in the US. At first disdainful of such a blatant racializing of his career, I watched with sadness as Teodros racialized himself as he lived the American way of life. For years, the two of us had walked as brothers and cousins.

Although only he is faithful to the teachings of Orthodox Christianity, we were both baptized in that church and used to laugh at the Greek character of his name. We were alternatively the two Greeks or the two Africans (since my mother was born in Cairo). Yet as his academic career became racialized, even our relationship was affected. One bad night, he even dared to call me white, for no fault of my own except for being part of the American context that offered him only opportunities to teach about race.

In my own work, I have continually encountered the failure of legislative bodies to rule on behalf of the people. In the US, most congress people and senators are multimillionaire lawyers beholden to corporate lobbyists and the Pentagon. Feeding at the trough of the public treasury, these lawmakers are little more than tax takers, standing in a long line with many medical doctors who seek to milk the cash cow of American citizenry for all they can get away with. At the front of the line stood war profiteer and former vice-president Richard Cheney, engorging himself from public monies as he continued to reap millions from Halliburton—whose contribution to the unnecessary war in Iraq is better known than its work for British Petroleum in constructing the failed oil well in the Gulf of Mexico. Zionist control of the US Congress leaves the interests of ordinary Americans far behind those of the citizens of Israel—a state whose theocratic core is far astray from the ideal foundation of secular democracy.

European philosophers of the 17th and 18th centuries sought to understand the structure of individual thought and to classify it according to its various dimensions and historical epochs. Using a similar analytical method, I seek in my own books to comprehend social movements as the logical process which unfolds within the praxis of thousands—and sometimes millions—of people as they rise up to change their lives. As German philosophers of the 18th century sought to uncover the structure and content of European ideas as they emerged in theory, I seek to portray the internal development and aspirations of popular movements as they are revealed in practice. In my view, people's collective praxis contains an unfolding logic, in which the innermost desires of ordinary people are revealed, and the specific character of freedom is defined. People's uprisings, such as those I explore in the global movement of 1968 and more recent Asian history, constitute the concrete realization of liberty—particularly during events like general strikes, uprisings, popular insurrections, and social revolutions. In the essays that follow, Kiros explores theories that deal with many of these very same questions. In so doing, he contributes to freedom's enduring struggle against dictatorship and oligarchy.

PREFACE
BY LEWIS GORDON

What is freedom without a home? What is a home without the conditions by which one could be "at home"? What are ideas without the affective force of the heart? And what is thought without a relationship to fellow human beings?

Teodros Kiros, a philosopher born in Ethiopia and educated in the United States, offers poignant response to these questions in this series of philosophical essays offered to the people of his beloved homeland. As an exile, and in spite of his American citizenship, he faces the impositions of limits on his speech akin to those on a guest. The prejudices of American society leave no room otherwise. To speak with fearless speech (what ancient Greeks called *parrhesia*), Kiros must write, at least in political terms, about Ethiopia.

The Ethiopian people, Kiros insists, pressed under the heels of oligarchy and brutal militarism, are homeless in their own country. Justice, he argues, is the missing element; justice is the demand for setting things right at home. This primary virtue of social institutions, as John Rawls claimed and Kiros concurs, calls for a fair share through which the least advantaged people of Ethiopia can be better off and through which all Ethiopians can be afforded greater liberties. Kiros calls this radical democracy.

To be moved by justice is, according to Kiros, to listen to the calling, the rhythmic force and intellectual affect, of the heart. In this core of the human spirit is, also, the rallying cry of justice. In radical democracy, justice and action meet.

Radical democracy is the admission that no human being really stands alone. To be is to live in relation to others, to understand how fellow human beings offer each other the social world in which the self faces meaning. This realization brings us full circle. Home is, after all, where one belongs. Kiros's love for Ethiopia occasions this reaching out to his fellow Ethiopians.

Home is, however, not only a place. It is also the ideas by which we are able to live. For Kiros, these ideas come from the best of two worlds: The ancient Egyptian understanding of *ma'at* (meaning, among other things, balance and things being in their right place), continued in the modern Ethiopian thought of Zara Yacob, and its transformation in Greek antiquity into what became known as justice, continued in the recent majestic effort of John Rawls and, as Kiros shows here, those influenced by him.

Kiros and I have had many conversations on Rawls, with whom he had conversed over the years at Harvard. Rawls basically argued for a more decent society where people are free to follow their pursuits and no one is left to fall below material levels necessary to live a life with dignity. I have no quarrel with that. The problem, I often clarified, was that most of the people in power and who are most advantaged by injustice in most societies appear very decent when we spend time with them. They go to places like Harvard and Oxford, send their children there, and often nod in agreement with such principles. Then, in positions of leadership, they face utilitarian or, as they see it, "practical" or "pragmatic" realities.

The difficult question is the relation of politics to ethics. Philosophers love ethics because their ultimate weapon is the persuasiveness of their arguments. Politicians despise philosophers for that reason. Philosophers demand the legitimating practices necessary, as Hannah Arendt argued, for the transformation of force into power. But can ethics alone occasion the transformation of force into power?

Rawls, as we know, argued that where his two principles conflict, the first—the libertarian principle—should prevail. In recent times, that position has been made concrete in the ideology of neoliberalism, and the result is more radicalized inequalities. Nearly a century ago, Charles Houston, the famed legal mind behind the legal strategy of the lawyers that successfully argued against Jim Crow in the United States, had also formulated two principles of justice similar to Rawls's. Houston argued, however, that if the two principles were in conflict, the difference principle addressing the welfare of the least advantaged peoples should prevail. How can liberty make sense, he contended, when the material conditions to act upon it are out of reach? Without such, libertarian principles amount, simply, to words from those whose options are guaranteed. The closing paragraph of Kiros's book suggests his agreement with Houston.

Rawls, then, is not the legitimation of Kiros's thought here. He is an important interlocutor through which the demand for justice is contextualized.

Speaking of context, my ongoing dialogue with Kiros on philosophy and politics began in a symposium I had organized at Brown University when I was chairperson of Africana Studies there. That meeting, which led to his teaching in that department for several years, was devoted to explorations of the decolonization of thought under the auspice of postcolonial phenomenology. Among the ways in which thought is colonized is through assertions of false universality. Many African Diasporic peoples are led to believe, for instance, that to work through ideas from Africana intellectual traditions is to think through minor terms, through particulars instead of universal themes. To demonstrate their universality, some attempt to demonstrate their affinities with the white scholarship that rejects them. The error here is obvious: What are the justifications for the standards imposed by such critics?

An interrogation of such standards is necessary, including those by which African intellectuals have presumed their legitimacy. Immediately, one discovers that a tradition that demands such a radical questioning of standards holds a greater capacity for universal reflection than its critics. It is the praxis of decolonizing knowledge.

In writing to his Ethiopian sisters and brothers with the call to critical reflection on democratic participation and justice through drawing upon their creative resources and reflective judgment, Kiros is engaging in that radical reflective spirit of *universalizing praxis*. In this sense, in all his homes—in Ethiopian and North American thought—he exemplifies the value of fearless speech, and in so doing, speaks to us all.

ACKNOWLEDGEMENTS

I must thank my committed publisher Kassahun Checole, who has faith in my work and has to date published all my important philosophical work, and my work as a novelist. I am most grateful to him.

I must also thank Damola Ifaturoti, the senior editor who prevailed over my book on Zara Yacob and this present book with such care and devotion as well as Chris Stites who helped tremendously in the editing and composition, even contributing his own name to the acknowledgments.

I also thank Mary Dooley for her meticulous proofreading. Senait Kassahun helped me in ways which I cannot adequately describe.

I thank Amare Aregawi, the editor of the *Ethiopian Reporter*, who published the essays as weekly columns for five years. I also thank the editor of *Deki Alula*, where I had a weekly column where I developed the ideas on development for five years. Finally I thank Teocla Hagos, editor of *TecolaHagos.com* and Abraha Belay, editor of *Ethiomedia* for publishing the essays on Ethiopian matters.

Irele Abiola, Kwasi Wiredu, Paget Henry and Lewis Gordon's friendships have contributed to my maturity as a scholar and human being; I thank them dearly for attending to all my needs in these long years and lonely years of struggle.

Finally, my years of affiliation with Harvard's African and African American studies and The Du Bois Institute continues to be a source of joy and challenge. I thank Henry Louis Gates, a devoted supporter of my Scholarship.

INTRODUCTION

Philosophical Essays seeks to present the idea of democracy systematically beginning with the ancient philosophers and ending with the modern philosopher, John Rawls.

Democracy as we have come to know it is associated with the Greek Philosophers, Plato and Aristotle. The accepted view is that the idea of democracy originated with the Greeks and that democracy is exclusively European.

Although this is largely true, there is a sense in which it is misleading, which needs to be corrected by further analytic distinctions.

I modestly propose that democracy is both a formal idea and a lived idea. As a formal idea, it is true that Plato and Aristotle presented it to the world systematically by writing about it and by subjecting to a rigorous conceptual analysis; as a lived idea the ancient Egyptians and Asians and following them other African states lived it, as the activity of the people arriving at ideas, deciding matters, taking positions and justifying them through deliberation and participation, two cardinal features of the democracy idea.

In this sense, the democracy idea was formalized by Plato and Aristotle, but was a lived practice long before the Greek thinkers were born. The point is that whereas Plato and Aristotle wrote about the observed by raising the experience into a conceptual form, whereas the Egyptian priests, who were Plato's teachers, left their observation on the level of oral discourse, without taking it to the next level of textual documentation. Plato and Aristotle then effectively originated the formal idea, while the ancient Egyptians and later African states lived the idea. Of course, the same Egyptians maintained slaves as the Greeks did, in spite of their keen awareness of the democratic idea. In this sense, the democracy idea was formalized by Plato and Aristotle, but was a lived practice long before the Greek thinkers were born.

Plato and Aristotle made mighty contributions to the democracy project as a formal idea, as much as the Egyptian priests, under whom Plato studied, who lived the democratic idea, and discoursed about it, without elevating it to the textual level as Plato and Aristotle did. In this sense the popular view that both philosophy and philosophical discourses on democracy originated in Greece, and through it to European intellectual scene needs a reinterpretation.

However, these Philosophical essays are informed by the written discourses of the European imagination. They are attempts at representing the democratic gazes of the European classical and modern traditions to the Ethiopian world.

They are attempts at cross-cultural conversations via the diffusion of the democratic idea to readers who may benefit from them and be guided by them.

The essays below are written with the purpose of diffusing the democracy idea to a large audience in a lucid, intelligible and clear language that would appeal to an English reading audience. The essays were first written for an Ethiopian audience, most particularly university students who may not have the means to purchase the classical texts, which fortunately are available to Western student. The typical Ethiopian student is not so fortunate.

Given this existential fact, I try to make a meek attempt to solve this financial handicap by taking the risk of presenting the arguments of the philosophers to an Ethiopian audience, who are familiar but not knowledgeable about the democratic idea, as they ought to be, since Ethiopian politicians continue to claim that they " revolutionary democrats"

The Democracy project, as I called it, is devoted to the task of evaluating the claims of the revolutionary democrats. My purpose was twofold. On the one hand, I want to contribute to the education of Ethiopians on the democratic idea. On the other hand I want to expose the vacuity of revolutionary democracy through the prism of the democracy idea philosophically.

It is this gaze that guides my interpretive journey with Plato and Aristotle, past the modern period and onto the contemporary views of the late john Rawls.

The interpretive journey is keenly aware of the vastness of the project, the role of language in conveying the information to an Ethiopian audience. On the one hand, I had to please the academic audience and all those internationally acclaimed scholars who have written on democracy, volumes of books. I pay attention both to form and content. Given the needs of my audience, the form that I chose, and the weekly essay, in which I produced one essay, a week, carefully, slowly and patiently, presents the material in a journalistic manner. I took on themes that occupied tons of books in two or three pages of clear prose, without ever neglecting attention to content. I made every human attempt to guide the content with an easy form and to fill the form with substantive content. I leave it to the reviewers of the book, if I have succeeded in this challenging venture.

The essays appeared in Ethiopia's leading newspaper, The Ethiopian Reporter, every week for a period of two years, and I hope that the Ethiopian students and other English speaking readers who read the essays have benefitted from them.

The present book is a collection of those essays in its present form, so that those who have already read them could read them in a book form, and those who encounter them for the first time could read them afresh and be engaged by them.

There is no substitute to the reading of the original material for those who can afford to buy them. For those who are both financially unable and for those who have no time to read them whole, here is a book which they may consider purchasing, and which might satisfy their intellectual curiosity thought the form of the short essay. The essay can only wet their appetite but not fully satisfy them. A complete intellectual satisfaction can only be obtained by wrapping themselves with the original classics on the democracy idea.

1

INTRODUCING THE
DEMOCRACY PROJECT

In several essays I will examine the idea of democracy, a widely but imprecisely understood concept in Ethiopian political discourse. I should like contribute toward a modest understanding of a favorite idea. I will argue that at the minimum one can develop four kinds of democracy, which I call classical democracy, modern democracy, contemporary democracy and radical democracy. The first three are intertwined phases of democracy. The last one has yet to be theorized, as I modestly attempt in this year long Democracy Project, as I wish to call it.

In the powerful pages of *The Republic*, Plato introduces us to the various ways of the construction of regimes and personalities that govern them. We are asked to imagine the human soul to have three parts: reason, desire and appetites. The human soul then comes divided into three parts, just like regimes are governed by three dominant principles. There are those regimes that value reason, those that yearn for desire, and those that succumb to unruly appetites. The genuine leader, Plato instructs, like the psychologist ought to be keenly aware of human nature. The ruler must attend to the distribution of reason, desire and appetites in the constitution of the citizen. The goal of the well-governed regime ought to be the cultivation of harmonious regimes and well-balanced human souls. Plato then proceeds to construct the ups and downs of regimes by focusing on the ups and downs of human souls.

On the shores of classical Greece, the childhood home of humanity, arose a powerful philosopher, Plato, the brilliant student of Socrates, the wise thinker, the founder of philosophy, the lover of wisdom, who deeply thought about the idea of democracy. It was he who systematically developed forms of regimes or governments and corresponding kinds of personalities. These ideas are explored in his famous *Republic*.

The Republic is divided into ten books. Book Eight is devoted to the exploration of forms of regimes that are appropriate for human beings. Plato introduces us to five regime types and five political personalities:

- Aristocracy-Aristocrat-Knowledge
- Timocracy-Timocrat-Honor
- Oligarchy-Oligarch-Money
- Democracy-Democrat-Freedom
- Tyranny-Tyrant-Power

The aristocratic regime is governed by the principle of knowledge. The aristocrat is wise. She has a love of wisdom or knowledge. Wisdom is the ultimate goal of the aristocratic personality, who is appointed to lead the people. Her qualifications for leadership are predicated on the quality and quantity of wisdom; political wisdom. The aristocratic regime disseminates this ideal and it attempts to make it a hegemonic idea. Unfortunately, the regime does not succeed. The people have other competing values that they wish to cultivate. Consequently, the yearning for wisdom gives way to the aggressive entrance of honor. Honor displaces wisdom.

Timocracy replaces aristocracy; the timocrat takes the place of the aristocrat. Honor is the organizing principle of timocracy. In this regime, honor does become a hegemonic idea. The young and the old drink from it. Everyone lives for honor. The timocrat becomes the leader of his people. Because he possesses what they all secretly and not so secretly wish to have, they choose him to lead them. Children at a very young age were trained by their nurses to ridicule those who fail to buy honor though wealth. They would hear their mothers complain about the fathers who have not become market men. The impressionable would hear these remarks and resolve to become honorable. Through these ingenious ways honor comes to take philosophy's place. A new value system is introduced in the interstices of timocracy. The people come to realize the benefits of honor: wealth, power and prestige.

Children listen to their mothers and nannies at home bitterly complaining about failed fathers. The father is called slack and cowardly because he did not choose money-making as a vocation. Impressionable children grow up listening to these gossips, resenting their ill-spoken fathers. So they resolve to change the tide of their own paths away from virtue and integrity.

Their desiring part is fueled with the oil of money and fame. The desiring part is overwatered while the reasoning part, which was the virtue of the aristocrat, lies fallow, like a neglected field. The timocrat now becomes an oligarch.

Oligarchy is organized by the quest for money. Money displaces honor. The timocrat becomes an oligarch. Once this trend starts it is almost unstoppable. Plato writes, "From there they progress in money making, and the more honorable they consider it, the less honorable they consider virtue.

Or isn't virtue in tension with wealth, as though each were lying in the scale of a balance, always inclining in opposite directions?...Surely, when wealth and the wealthy are honored in the city, virtue and the good men are less honorable. What happens to be honored is practiced, and what is without honor is neglected" (*The Republic*, 551a-b, p. 228).

The love of victory and the honor that came with it is now replaced by the love of money and the value that is conferred on the wealthy. The poor man is dishonored. Begging and stealing become the poor man's ways. The wealthy produce new truth that humiliates and describes the poor.

The wealthy oligarch does not have a specialty. He is a jack of all trades. When mood moves him he doubles in all trades, including war making, about which he knows nothing. The oligarch's excessive desire comes at the expense of producing poverty, neighborhood thieves, cutpurses, temple robbers.

The streets of Addis are marked reminders of this reality. By the yardstick of life in Addis nothing seems to have changed. Rather, the question that Plato asked in *The Republic* remains puzzling.

FROM

The Ethiopian Reporter, July 3, 2001.

SOURCE

Allan Bloom, Ed, *The Republic of Plato*, New York: Basic Books 1968.

2

FROM OLIGARCHY TO DEMOCRACY

The oligarch's excessive love of money infuriates the demos (the people). Whereas the oligarch endows himself with luxuries and unnecessary commodities, the people are denied the fundaments of the body, necessary food, shelter and clothing. This situation of excess for the oligarch and deficiency for the people produces a tense situation, calling for radical political change in the wombs of oligarchy.

In Plato's words, "Then Democracy, I suppose, comes into being when the poor win, killing some of the others and casting out some, and share the regime and the ruling offices with those who are left on an equal basis; and, for the most part, the offices in are given by lot" (*The Republic*, 557a, p. 235).

Democracy is organized by the principle of freedom, and the democratic man keeps his guard down. He does not compromise his freedom. He is excessively free. His soul is unbalanced. There are factions and fractures in his soul. Reason is always on a holiday, and desire runs unchecked. The democratic man is a frightening man. Free speech and unruly desires govern his soul. He is undisciplined. Self-control is a foreign disposition to a democratic personality. In his soul, desire is at war with reason. Desire always wins.

The democratic regime houses all the other regimes. Aristocracy, timocracy and oligarchy freely float inside the democratic regime. The democratic personality pretends to be sometimes the lover of wisdom, the philosopher-king; at other times, he embraces the love of honor; frequently, he poses as an intimidating oligarch with wealth and honor. He desires all the other regimes. He becomes them all, like the jack of all trades and the master of none.

Plato ironically tells us that democracy is a sweet regime. Many multicolored, pretentious, ostensible lovers of equality are shamelessly drawn to it. The democrat does not distinguish necessary and unnecessary desire. He is a desiring being, pure and simple. As a many-colored man the democrat tries to please everyone, without loyalty to a single one.

For Plato, there are unnecessary and necessary desires. Unnecessary desires are those things we should not want, and we can train ourselves not to want them. Necessary are those desires that want us, or that we should want. Eating, for example, is a necessary desire, provided that we regulate the content by reason. Unfortunately, these distinctions are lost on the democrat. The democrat is a drone, argues Plato. He "is full of such pleasures and desires and is ruled by the unnecessary ones, while the stingy oligarch is ruled by the necessary ones" (*The Republic*, 559 d, p. 237).

How did democracy evolve out of oligarchy, and how did the oligarch become a democrat? Plato answers: "When a young man, reared as we were saying without just education and stingily, tastes the drone's honey, and has intercourse with fiery, clever beasts who are able to purvey manifold and subtle pleasures with every sort of variety, you presumably suppose that at this point he begins his change from an oligarchic regime within himself to a democratic one" (559e, p. 238). From this point onward, the democrat loses focus, confounds freedom with license and is saddled with insolence, wastefulness, anarchy, shamelessness and recklessness. The unnecessary desires overwhelm him. Drinking, listening to flute, idling at the gymnasium, flirting with philosophy become his daily habits.

The recent events in Ethiopia (the war against Eritrea) seem to illustrate the pervasive presence of self-serving oligarchs on whose victory at war had once been bestowed heavy honor. As recent events unfold, however, an obsessive quest for money has replaced the principle of honor. The modern Ethiopian state is now trembling because of this sudden shift that socialism had supposedly erased. So we were told by the powers to be. Soon did we discover that old habits never die, and that the perennial power of money has come in full swing now. We are on the verge of being swallowed by the excessive appetites of democratic men. The democratic regime is now waiting to be rescued by a powerful tyrant, who will deliver from the voracious appetites of democratic men, as Plato would have argued.

From

The Ethiopian Reporter, July 10, 2001

3

FROM DEMOCRACY
TO TYRANNY

Plato's major thesis about the human roots of domination is fully articulated in his truly stunning portrayal of the tyrannical disposition in human character found in the ninth book of *The Republic*. Plato's thesis may be summarized as follows.

For Plato, it is a democratic regime that becomes a necessary condition for the emergence of a tyrannical regime. Tyranny then is a negative value to the extent that it is a transformation from democracy. Democracy itself, which for Plato is a regime where liberty is abused, is also a negative value. Plato characterized tyranny in this way. Central to a deep understanding of the tyrant—someone whose self-constitution involves the need to dominate others as well as his or her helplessness due to domination by the external force of unnecessary pleasures—is Plato's unique insight into the nature of desire.

In a major passage, Plato wrote:

> Of the unnecessary pleasures and desires, there are, in my opinion, some that are hostile to law and that probably come to be in everyone; but, when checked by the laws and the better desires, with the help of argument, in some human beings they are entirely gotten rid of or

only a few weak ones are left, while in others stronger and more numerous ones remain.

"Which ones do you mean?" he said.

"Those," I said, "that make up in sleep when the rest of the soul—all that belongs to the calculating, tame, and ruling part of it—slumbers, while the beastly and wild part, gorged with food or drink, is skittish and, pushing sleep away, seeks to go and satisfy its dispositions. You know that is such a state it dares to do everything as though it were released from, and rid of, all shame and prudence. And it does not shy from attempting intercourse, as it supposes, with a mother or anyone else at all—human beings, gods, and beasts, or attempting any foul member at all, and there is no food from which it abstains. And in a word, it omits no act of folly or shamelessness." (*The Republic of Plato*, (571 c-d, PP,251-52).

For Plato, human beings are desiring beings who gravitate toward the apparently good and move away from the apparently nondesirable (or bad). This movement constitutes a major portion of human activities. When human beings move toward the desirable, however, they generally do not pause to critically and judiciously evaluate the merits of the different objects of desire. Plato makes the major observation that although human beings tend to tenaciously follow their instincts when they seek to gratify the objects of their desires, because desiring as such is "natural," it does not necessarily follow that they are right to do so. Rather, Plato seeks to awaken us to the radical idea that desiring each and everything without making a self-generated decision to examine the nature of desire itself is ultimately destructive. Yet we often choose not to open our power of inquiry to the problem of desire.

For those who wish to be thinking people, human existence is too precious for them to let themselves be guided by the meandering of goal-less desires. Existence is generally goal-directed (for example, toward happiness), as are the desires upon which existence is anchored. Rarely, however, are we aware of this basis for our existence.

For Plato, not all desires are equally admirable. Some are excellent, others are very good, and still others are simply bad. Some desires are absolutely necessary for our human existence: food, shelter, clothing are good examples; and some other desires, for example, excessive alcohol, drugs and the like, are objectively harmful to the human body and spirit. Those desires that are excellent are so because they have become subjected to the regulative direction of self-imposed law. Desires that cannot be directed by the regulative power of self-imposed law necessarily become bad, as do the characters of human beings that live their lives chaotically.

Plato contends that the desires that destroy human beings are those that are particularly active during sleep. In the sleeping state, anything is desirable. The objects of desire in the Dream State are boundless, lawless, shameless, ungovernable, impervious to regulated direction by reason or the solemn state of inquiry. What is even more frightening is the fact that these desires feel wild, and ruthless, even to those who relish the feeling of freedom released by the demonic charm of boundless desires. There are unnatural desires that need to be controlled.

Furthermore, "a man becomes tyrannical in the precise sense when, either by nature or by his practices or both, he has become drunken, erotic and melancholic." (Ibid, 573 c, p, 253). The tyrant would pursue the most unnatural desires when fancy and an exaggerated need compel him. Thus Plato writes, "Is your opinion that for the sake of a newly-formed lady friend and unnecessary concubine such a man will strike his old friend and necessary mother, or that for the sake of a newly-found and unnecessary father who is no longer in the bloom of youth and is the oldest of friends, and that he will enslave his parents to them if he should bring them into the same house" (Ibid, 574b.c, p, 255)

Drunkenness, eros and melancholy are human vices for Plato. They are vices that describe the fallen state to which the tyrannical self enters when it surrenders its will to unnatural desires—desires that deliberately and shamelessly transgress the boundaries set by the inquiring or reasonable self. Drunkenness, eros, and melancholy are either products of nature, in which case they are outside human control but themselves become controlling forces, or are constructs of habitual practice, in which case they are directly but over a long period of time caused by human beings against their own selves. In short, the vices of drunkenness, eros and melancholy are both natural and social. Naturalness and sociability are deeply involved in what humans do and do not do, what humans are and are not, what human beings have actually become and can overcome.

Plato characteristically vacillates between nature, the permanently unchangeable power, and the social, the ceaselessly in flux fluid, dynamic—product of conscious human choice.

The desires then are potentially deep sources of a tragic form of life, found, for example, in the classic Greek literature of the Oedipus myth, where human values are shamelessly transgressed for the sake of lustful desires seeking an outlet in raw sexuality. For Plato, the desires are also equally healthy wells of a longing for a peaceful life. This life contains moments of eros and aphrodisia, love and sexuality, which consummate in the births of human beings, destined to propagate the human species. This form of life, neither tragic nor paradoxical but a healthy blend of the two moments, is what thinkers of all ages have longed for, so far to no avail. The wondering, the quest, the refusal to dream and not to dream are all bound up with the potential of human desires, the potential of human beings to destroy, regress, imagine and create—imagination to construct and the will to destroy. Drunkenness, eros and melancholy are thus destructive powers as well as constructive human gifts, of which Plato was critically aware.

For Plato, drunken and erotic tyrants are the worst enemy of their own selves. They do not have a friendly attitude toward their own selves; they do not profoundly love themselves. Because they are not friends to themselves, we can safely infer that they are equally incapable of entering into friendship with other human beings. Plato put it thus: "Therefore, they live their whole life without ever being friend of anyone, always one's master of another's slave. The tyrannical nature never has a task of freedom or true friendship" (Ibid, 576 a, p, 256).

Plato and others have provided some important insights about the nature of domination. Plato is right when he asserts that tyrants are neither free nor friendly. Freedom and friendship are foreign to their character. They are nonvalues to tyrants. At a minimum, tyrants must either deny or completely dominate others in order that they may feel free. They in turn, although not consciously, are dominated by the thoughtless and irrational desire to dominate others. Dominating others is a necessary condition for tyrants to feel free. Note that for tyrants, what is really important is not that they are actually free as much as that they feel free. The freedom that they feel is actually the absence of freedom of those others who are dominated by their experience. Tyrants' freedom is so dominated by thoughtlessness that they are prevented from ever disengaging themselves from the will to dominate in order to consider why someone would dominate others.

For Plato, the structure of a tyrant's character is the key we must turn to enter their inner depths. Three foundational pillars uphold the soul or psyche of the tyrannical inner regime: reason and unreason with the desire suspended in between. A mature and truly balanced character must have a well-blended mix of these three foundations. A character can be said to be reasonable if his or her desire for gain, honor and prudence is fundamentally dominated not by gain or honor, but rather by the erotic desire for prudence. Such a character is considered to be the true aristos (king). He or she is capable of intimate self-governance and can correctly choose the appropriate wants and subsequently satisfy the objects of human desire. The kingly or aristocratic inner regime is guided by prudence; gain and honor are consequently subordinate to prudence. The inner regime is not mesmerized by gain and honor, as is the tyrannical inner regime.

The tyrant is the exact opposite of the aristocrat. Whereas prudence or reason captivates the aristocrat, the tyrant is intoxicated with the desires for unlimited monetary gain or the honor of power, and an imprudence that erases the power of choice has been erased. The intoxication with gain and honor leads the tyrant to reduce all relationships with others, including friends and loved ones, to means.

Tyrants would even enslave themselves to others by belittling themselves if the others could be made to serve for their well-planned future scheme. For the tyrant, human beings are not intrinsically lovable or worthy of love. They are either useful or useless instruments for his own pleasure.

Tyrants are not free. They are slaves of gain, money and status—each of which germinates from the depth of the pillar of desire undirected by reason. Tyrants do not use their critical powers of prudence or inquiry; therefore they are inexperienced in dispassionately thinking about the objects of desire. Any desired object is impudently and thoughtlessly pursued. Thus, in the tyrant's eyes, even one's own mother could be a sexually desired object, if that enables the tyrant to get his or her way. The values of right and wrong, good and evil, justice and injustice, friendliness and hate are all judged as equal, without intrinsic differences that stir the human mind and heart to be deeply concerned about the human condition. The tyrant unconcerned about the well-being of others cannot be moved by anything except gain.

Tyrants cannot enter into friendship because true friendship demands love, compassion, patience, limitless time and, above all, a sense of justice. The tyrant who is enslaved by self-centered desires cannot provide other-oriented virtues such as love, compassion and patience. Only those who are great can be compassionate toward others when it is demanded from them. The tyrant cannot give either freedom or friendship to others precisely because he/she has never experienced the flares of freedom and friendship.

Tyrants are tragic figures in that they have never loved their own selves. Tyrants experience life not as self-empowerment but strictly as the will to power. Government through Bonapartism has recently displayed this dangerous fashion of exacting consensus, when reason utterly fails. Ethiopians are instructed to be cautious of this unwanted development of negative discourse of tyranny.

FROM
Ethiopian Reporter, July 17, 2001.

4

Revisiting Classical Democracy Through Aristotle's Eyes

The democracy of Aristotle is similar to Plato's in that it too appends tremendous power to reason in the soul structure of the democratic personality. Also, a harmonious soul is superior to a factious one. Both Plato and Aristotle shared this ideal.

Balance in all things and a moderate fabric are the keys to a healthy city—this is Plato's central insight. There are crucial differences as well. As we recall, Plato was extremely critical of democracy. For him, democracy allowed much freedom, unregulated by reason. The democrat abused the ideal of freedom in the name of doing as he pleased, and this infuriated Plato, the rationalist. In contrast, Aristotle tolerates the abuse of freedom, up to a point. To be sure, he too does not think that democracy is the best regime. He chooses it as the better evil, and also because, for Aristotle, democracy offers a model of balance.

Democracy, as Aristotle theorizes it, offers the avoidance of excesses and deficiencies of values, such as freedom and equality, to mention a few. It cuts right in the middle of excess, such as freedom as license and coercion to do what others want you to do. Or, say, excess such as equality and a deficiency such as inequality.

Aiming at the median is an Aristotelian ideal. The median in turn is that point that stands between an excess and deficiency. The median is the centerpiece of Aristotle's *Nichomachean Ethics*.

The median in the distribution of virtues—all virtues, such as courage, justice and truth—is the organizing principle of democracy, when it is so idealized. In Aristotle's words, "democracy exists whenever the free born is sovereign, and oligarchy, whenever the rich are in control" (*Politics*, p. 163). All that one needs to be is freely born, to qualify for an office. Slaves are unqualified because they are not born free. Otherwise, observed Aristotle, "we should have an oligarchy if offices were distributed on the basis of stature [as they are said to be in Ethiopia]" (Ibid, p, 164). For Aristotle, free birth is the essence of democracy. That is the first natural property of personality. By this measure, the poorest person, provided that he or she is free born, can run for public office. Wealth is an unnecessary secondary quality, whereas freedom is a necessary and sufficient quality for citizenship.

Furthermore, for Aristotle, freedom by definition assumes equality of beginnings. Freedom respects and endorses equality. By virtue of the fact one is born free, then one is bound to think that he or she is everybody's equal. Free persons have the same point of origin and the same prospects of success or failure in the social lottery of life. Freedom breeds equality, and equality contributes toward the sustenance of freedom.

There are varieties of democracies, reports Aristotle. The first variety is democracy with equality and freedom; the second is the type that assigns offices to the propertied; the third assigns offices to those who descend from notable families; the fourth assigns offices to the incontestably free born; the fifth, like the fourth, cherishes free descent, but descent is determined not by an objective law, but by the passions of the people.

Aristotle is disturbed by the fifth variety. The people sometimes become autocratic and do not deliberate well. Aristotle prefers democracies governed by supremely objective law, rather than the whims of the demos (the people). The people err. The law can be written to err less. He warns repeatedly against the people becoming autocratic and demagogues. Demagoguery can easily lead to oligarchy, he observes. Unlike Plato, Aristotle does not think that democracy can degenerate into tyranny, rather, it degenerated into oligarchy. He writes, "The demagogues anxious to have an excuse for confiscating the property, drove a number of the notables into exile, with the result that the exiles become so numerous that they effected their return, defeated the people in battle, and established an oligarchy" (p. 215).

FROM

The Ethiopian Reporter, July 24, 2001.

SOURCES

Aristotle, *Nicomachean Ethics*, Englewood, NJ: Prentice Hall, 1968.

Aristotle, *Politics*, London: Pelican Classics, 1968.

5

FROM THE STATE OF NATURE TO SOCIETY: THE COMMONWEALTH

In interpreting Thomas Hobbes, I argue that the state of nature is a state of war, and that that state of war can be averted from leading into full-fledged war, if a sovereign ruler of a functional government is created. For Hobbes (1588-1679), government is a contrivance, a necessity, precisely because "men are not angels." Good laws must control their evil ways, that they may be compelled to follow, for their own sake.

Man is forced out of the state of nature, because he is keenly aware of his contentious and cantankerous nature. Once he forces himself out, he may obtain peace in return. In return to leaving the state of nature, man will be rewarded by becoming a subject of a government. Man desires peace, but he does not know how to obtain it. His violent nature understands only war, not peace. Government, however, can show him how to live peacefully under the tutelage of the laws of nature. The move from the state of nature to society constitutes a major event in the evolution of human history, concludes Hobbes.

As Hobbes put it, "The final cause, End, or Design of men (who naturally love liberty, and Dominion over others) in the introduction of that restraint upon themselves (in which we see them live in commonwealths) is the foresight of their own preservation" (*Leviathan*, p. 228). Self-preservation is the first law of nature. Although man is born violent, nasty and brutish, he still desires peace. Tragically, his desire notwithstanding, he does not know how to attain it.

There are other laws of nature that man can be trained to internalize as a duty. They are justice, equity, modesty, mercy and doing to others as would be done to you. Man can be socialized to make these moral properties his very own. Man is ultimately malleable, argues Hobbes. These laws are not man's natural properties. They are properties that education can inoculate to man as a citizen and subject of the state.

Furthermore, these laws can also be part of a covenant between man and man. As Hobbes puts it, "I authorize and give my right of governing myself, to this man, or to this assembly of men, on this condition, that thou give up their right to him, and authorize all his actions in like manner... this done, the multitude so united is called a Common-Wealth, in Latin, CIVITAS" (p. 227). This is how government is generated, according to Hobbes.

The multitude thus convinced can rationally exchange their natural liberties for political liberties that can effectively defend them against their violent self. The form of the government that can actuate this change is left unspecified.

All that Hobbes argues is that whatever form of government men choose, they need to establish a powerful sovereign that will give them peace and security. This principle applies to aristocracy, oligarchy and democracy. For my purposes it is the application to the democracy project that concerns me.

In democracy, the citizens are bearers of rights and liberties. Hobbes calls them the liberties of subjects. These liberties are absolute. No sovereign can violate them.

By this standard, the recent violent death of the forty-one students in Ethiopia (2005) is a violation of the liberties of the subjects. This is particularly true since the demands of the students were reasonable and attainable, through political discourse. Violence was used to obliterate the voice of the young subjects. By liberty Hobbes says: "Liberty or Freedom, signifies [properly] the absence of opposition; (by opposition, I mean external impediments of motion) and may be applied no less to Irrational, and Inanimate creatures, than to Rational" (p. 261).

Thus defined, the first liberty of the subject is the freedom to do as one pleases with one's own body. The subject is also equally free to use his or her reasoning power to decide right and wrong. Finally, the subject can assume liberties about which the official law of the land is silent. Hobbes was so perceptive that he went so far to argue that "And in some places of the world, men have the liberty of many wives: in other places, such liberty is not at all allowed."

The democratic moments in Hobbes are informed by a delicate balance between the liberty of the subjects and the rights of the state to regulate some of the liberties, if they endanger the lives of the subjects themselves, given the violent nature of men. Hobbes gives enough liberties to the subjects, and at the same allows the state to exercise its own liberties, for the sake of preserving the commonwealth.

The Hobbes that I have interpreted here is considerably less authoritarian than the popular Hobbes. I have deliberately extracted the democratic sensibilities of Hobbes, without denying the often-noted authoritarian streaks in Hobbesianism. The democratic moments are carried further in the democratic visions of John Locke, whom I will interpret in the next essay.

FROM

The Ethiopian Reporter, August 15, 2001.

SOURCE

Thomas Hobbes, *Leviathan*, London: Pelican Classics, 1968.

6

JOHN LOCKE AND MODERN LIBERAL DEMOCRACY

John Locke (1632-1704) lived during trying times. Like Hobbes before him, Locke's vision of government is guided by a vision of human possibilities. His vision is informed by a deep understanding of human nature. As one of his able interpreters, Professor Lamprecht noted, "Locke lived through one of the most troubled periods in English history. He witnessed the hard struggle between Charles I and Parliament, the rise to power of the Presbyterians and Independents, the execution of Charles, the rule of Cromwell, the restoration and reign of Charles II and James II, the Glorious Revolution of 1688, and the constitutional settlement under William and Mary" (Locke, *Selections from Political Writings*, p, v).

Locke had the rare gift of weighing them all, navigating through rich political positions and staking out his own stand judiciously and intelligently. Tolerance was his trademark. That is how Locke sought to reserve the great debates in modern English political and church history. Many times he was embroiled in these controversies. Like Zara Yacob, the Ethiopian philosopher, Locke's contemporary, he too was drawn to debates, and like him he was always used the light of reason to articulate his own position, without tutelage to any power.

FROM

The *Ethiopian Reporter*, August 22, 2001.

SOURCE

John Locke, *Second Treatise of Government*, New York: Pelican, 1968.

7

JOHN LOCKE AND THE STATE OF NATURE

Locke asks, "What is man? What is man capable of?" (Locke, p.119) Answering that requires entering into the labyrinth of the state of nature. For Locke the state of nature is not the state of war, as it was for Hobbes. Man in the state of nature lives in perfect freedom. Free is man in this state to decide what he should want and not want, possess and not possess, within the bounds of nature. The state of nature is also the state of equality. Every person is the equal of another. Under this state of equality, men and women share things without seeking to dominate or conquer the other. It is the state of plenty.

To say that this is a state of liberty is not to assume that it is a state of license. For example, man has no liberty to take his own life. There is an implicit law of nature that prohibits man from exercising that freedom against himself.

One such law argues Locke, "teaches all equal and independent, no one ought to harm another in his life, health, liberty or possessions, for men being all the workmanship of one omnipotent and infinitely wise maker...they are his property" (*Second Treatise of Government*, p.118).

Man's freedom to own his body does not include the freedom to take it away. His body was given to him so that he can properly use it. There are proper and improper uses of that body. The first principle teaches that man cannot take away what is not properly his. Locke's view is this is an improper use of freedom.

Similarly, the law of nature commands all of us to preserve our lives, and refrain from harming others. Those who are able to face the transgressors, such as robbers and killers, must punish whatever is found disturbing the tranquility and peace that we deserve. Writes Locke "thus it is everyman in the state of Nature has a power to kill a murderer, both to deter others from doing the like injury (which no reparation can compensate) by the example of the punishment that attends it from everybody" (p. 119).

In the state of nature, every person has an executive power by which to enforce reasonable and proper laws of nature. True, some people do abuse this power by revenging against those they do not like, when they catch them. Equally true as we learned from Hobbes is the fact that men are partial toward themselves and those like them. Locke's answer to this problem is the argument that it is the duty of a good government to write laws that could justly punish this unwonted impartiality and revenge. Punishment must always equal the degree of the crime.

For Locke, the state of nature is separate from the state of war. As we recall, the great Hobbes confounded these two realms. Locke is at pains to separate them. Locke preaches that the state of nature, contra Hobbes, is a state of good will, peace, mutual assistance and preservation. The state of war, on the other hand, is a state of enmity, destruction, malice and violence. Locke writes, "it is only the want of a common judge with authority puts all men in a state of nature; force without right upon a man's person makes a state of war both where there is, and is not, a common judge" (p.119).

For Locke, natural man is peaceful and free. Modern man becomes violent once he enters civil society as a subject and citizen. It is society that corrupts his good will and peaceful disposition. In this Hobbes and Locke are at loggerheads. Locke is much closer to Jean Jacques Rousseau than he is to Hobbes, as I will argue in the next essay.

FROM

The Ethiopian Reporter, August 29, 2001.

SOURCE

John Locke, *Second Treatise of Government*, New York: Pelican, 1968.

8

JOHN LOCKE ON GOVERNMENT

Men are equal, free and independent in the state of nature. So when they decide to enter society, it is done through the consent of everyman so as to secure the preservation of their property and to enjoy comfortable, safe and peaceful living. The reason behind this move is, argues Locke, in the state of nature man's enjoyment of his rights is insecure and inconsistent. It can be taken away easily.

So man reasons that it is to his advantage to found government that would provide him the much-needed security, because man is, as we learned from Thomas Hobbes, diffident. From which emerges Locke's famous proposition "The great and chief end, therefore, of men uniting into commonwealth, and putting themselves under gov't, is the preservation of their property" (*Second Treatise*, paragraph 124).

Second, government provides its citizens with an impartial judge who can settle disputes; and finally, government provides an official executive power that can enforce decisions. Once men decide to enter society, they give up their natural liberties and rights in exchange for greater rights and liberties they can attain in society, systematically secured by government. These rights and liberties are safeguarded through the division of power into three chambers: legislative, executive and federative. Each branch has a specific function.

The legislative chamber makes laws. It is the supreme power. This fountain of power makes the governing laws of society. The power of this body cannot be willfully transferred to any other body. By appointing individuals, the people, the source of sovereignty, ask representatives to make laws.

The power of executing laws originating in the legislature is enforced by the executive power. The executive chamber cannot make laws. It executes laws that are already made and promulgated in the Constitution.

The Federative branch declares war and peace, founds leagues and alliances, and determines all the other relevant transactions and communities without commonwealth.

We see here how carefully power is neatly divided among diverse bodies. Unlike Hobbes, who confounds the distinctions, Locke shrewdly fragments sovereignty, fearful that one powerful tyrant, as in Plato's *Republic* could easily usurp too much power, by intimidating the people and manipulating the law of the land.

For Locke, ultimate power must be placed in the hands of the people, via empowering the legislative branch. Locke was so aware of the potential abuse of power in the hands of the executive that he wrote: "if the executive power, being possessed of the force of the commonwealth, shall make use of that force to hinder the meeting and acting of the legislative, when the original constitution or the public exigencies require it. I say, using force upon the people, without authority, and contrary to the trust put in him that does so is in a state of war with the people" (para. 155).

By this precise democratic measure the recent use of executive power against the representatives of the people in Ethiopia was a gross violation of the separation of powers. The executive branch usurped power, through what has been called "Bonapartism." This is not the place to fully analyze this unconstitutional measure. I will return to this theme, when I theorize about contemporary revolutionary democracy in Ethiopia. Future essays will continue to interpret the meaning and scope of the idea of democracy.

FROM

The Ethiopian Reporter, August 29, 2001.

SOURCE

John Locke, *Second Treatise of Government*, New York: Pelican, 1968.

9

JEAN JACQUES ROUSSEAU ON THE SOCIAL CONTRACT

Rousseau, a controversial and eloquent figure of the 18th century, was born on June 28, 1712 and died on July 2, 1778. His reflections on the foundations of government and society begin with the justly famous proposition, "Man is born free and everywhere he is in chains" (Rousseau, *The Social Contract,* Chapter 1, pg.2). To the obvious question, if man was born free, how did he become chained? the philosopher candidly answers, "I do not know."

The first and oldest form of society is, declares Rousseau, the family. That is the first major unit of society. The family lasts as long as the children are there. Once the children leave that unit is dissolved. The children move on to be the subjects and citizens of the largest form of society. Rousseau learns from Hobbes and Locke that self-preservation is the first law of nature, which everybody observes. The child who is a member of the family, and whose life is preserved by the parents, moves out of that unit when he comes out of age and joins society. There lest he is destroyed, he follows the first law of nature and preserves his life.

However, the family continues to be a viable model of society. The head of the state continues to resemble the head of the family. The people resemble the members of the family. Born free and equal, like the members of the family, they obey their rulers only because they foresee an advantage, not because they are forced.

For Rousseau obedience cannot be commanded; like love, obedience must be freely chosen. The main difference between the family and society is that the family is bound by love, whereas society is held together by duty, by a self-willed covenant.

Aristotle and following him Plato wrongly thought that humans are not equal. Wrong, Rousseau argues. Like Locke before him, Rousseau believes that humans are born as equals, like family members. It is society that enslaves them and makes them unequal. As he put it, "Force made the first slaves; and their cowardice perpetuates their slavery" (*Social Contract*, chapter 2).

Those who yield to slavery are not giving their will or consent to the condition of slavery. No. They are yielding to the fear of force as violence, argues Rousseau. Right does not command obedience. It forces it as if it is exacting obedience. Force postpones disobedience, but it never, never produces objective obedience, not even as duty. Those who obey their masters and tyrants do so spitefully. The moment force disappears, disobedience immediately follows, precisely because the obedience was not produced by reason but was nothing more than the effect of power as force, not power as reason. Therefore those who force obedience have no right to do so, nor are those who are obeying have the duty to obey. Force does not make right, is Rousseau's extraordinary conclusion.

Therefore he continues, "Since no man has any natural authority over his fellows, and since force alone bestows no right, all legitimate authority among men must be based on covenants" (chapter 4).

Such a covenant needs a form of political association, and Rousseau says, "How to find a form of association which will defend the person and goods of each member with the collective force, and under which each individual, while uniting himself with the others, obeys no one but himself, and remains as free as before" (chapter 6).

Indeed the philosopher's life-long commitment was the production of precisely that appropriate social contract founded by freely and equally born human beings to securely preserve life, liberty and happiness. The people as the supreme power, the legislators, the makers of good laws, must determine the precise content of this association. In this Rousseau is indebted to Locke, whose theories of the functions of the legislators I examined.

Rousseau goes much further than Locke, however. This pact can work only if the people give up their individual liberties to a sovereign power, such as a single ruler, or a political party, which will in turn invoke these liberties anew as the liberties of the citizen body. The whole community becomes the sovereign body to which the otherwise lone individual alienates his freedom. All individuals do the same. In this way no one feels compelled to give up anything, since what was previously the individual's is now the community's. The impartiality and fairness that is potentially implicit in the whole community now exchange the partiality inherent in the state of nature.

When the community is thus deprived of inessentials, argues Rousseau, what is left is "Each one of us puts into the community his person and all his powers under the same direction of the General Will; and as a body, we incorporate every member as an indivisible part of the whole" (chapter 7).

The nature of the general will and the kind of government Rousseau favors will be the subject of the next essay.

FROM

The Ethiopian Reporter, September 9, 2001.

SOURCE

Jean Jacques Rousseau, *Social Contract*, New York: Henry Regnery Co. ed. Wilmore 1954.

10

THE GENERAL WILL AND THE SOCIAL CONTRACT

The general will always appeals to and expresses the common good, the good of all citizens of a state. The general will is that which unites all those diverse interests and passions of citizens into a single whole, a whole composed of particular interests generalized into the form of a common good.

Sovereignty then is nothing more than the exercise of the general will. This will, argues Rousseau, cannot be alienated or separated into unrelated compartments of disparate functions, such as the legislative and executive chambers. It is indivisible and inalienable. These are its natural properties.

Power, as we learned from Locke, can be delegated, can be systematically divided into the legislative, executive and federative functions. In this Rousseau agrees with Locke. But Rousseau emphatically and distinctly argues that the general will, as the will of the pesople, cannot be so divided.

The general will is indivisible, therefore, cannot be divided or alienated from the body of the citizens.

Of course, the general will as the collective will of the people can err, because its carriers, the people, are flawed and finite. They make mistakes. The general will errs when incipient forms of factions and sectional associations divorced from the common good invade it.

The ongoing uncovering of corruption in Ethiopian social and political life is a particularly fitting example of a general will contaminated by particular interests advancing their agendas at the expense of the people, the fountains of sovereignty.

FROM
The Ethiopian Reporter, September 12, 2001.

11

THE ORIGIN OF INEQUALITIES

Why do we have inequalities, asked Rousseau? This question has haunted a long list of brilliant philosophers, but none of them provided the original insight of Rousseau. His eloquence and his depth were unparalleled in his time.

For Rousseau, there are two kinds of inequalities: natural or physical inequality, and moral or political inequality. The cause of the first is nature; hence our physical differences are visible in age, bodily strength, health, the quality of the mind and the soul. The cause of the second is human convention and the consent of men. Moral inequality is manifest in the differences of wealth, power and honor. Those very passions that Hobbes argued are natural. For Rousseau, they are conventional. They are not the qualities of natural man but rather the attributes of modern man. Rousseau is interested in examining the cause of moral and political inequalities, since he cannot do anything about natural inequalities.

Natural man is simple. Rousseau imagined him satisfying his thirst at the first brook; his hunger at the first oak; his bed under the shade of a tree. Thus so easily did he satisfy his fundamental needs. Contra Hobbes, natural man is not brutish but kind, not nasty but compassionate, not aggressive but peaceful. Nastiness, brutishness and the shortness of life are not the attributes of natural man; they are rather distinct qualities of modern man.

Thus writes Rousseau, "the Caribbeans, who have as yet of all deviated from the state of nature, being in fact the most peaceable of people in their amours, and the least subject to jealousy, thought they live in a hot climate which seems always to inflame the passions" (*Discourse on the Origin and Foundation of the Inequality of Mankind*, p. 425).

He concludes, "Man in the state of nature, wandering up and down the forests, without industry, without speech, and without home, an equal stranger to war and all ties, neither standing in need of his fellow creatures nor having any desire to hurt them...being self-sufficient and subject to so few passions...that he felt only his actual necessities" (p. 425).

Following Locke, he argues that the founder of civil society is the first man, who "enclosed a piece of ground, bethought of himself of saying, this is mine, and found people simple enough to believe him" (p. 427).

This impostor is the founder of private property as well. Once society was founded on this dubious foundation, man was compelled to compete and trust every other man, thus reproducing Hobbes' man. Indeed modern man had to fend for himself to protect his private property, and founds government to preserve his life and property. Both Hobbes and Locke were describing modern man, not natural man. They found man in his corrupt form, and not in his original form, argues Rousseau.

Inventiveness, industriousness, technology, deceit and manipulation are some of the qualities modern man was compelled to develop after the fall from peacefulness and controlled aggression. Once these qualities were firmly placed in society they seamlessly led to the entrenchment of inequalities in wealth, power and honor. For Rousseau modern liberal democracy finds its beginnings in the seeming naturalness of these inequalities.

FROM

The Ethiopian Reporter, September 19, 2001.

SOURCE

Jean Jacques Rousseau, *Discourse On The Origin of Human Inequalities* (New York: 1973).

12

DAVID HUME ON THE SOCIAL CONTRACT

In modern political philosophy three giants, Hobbes, Locke and Rousseau, as I argued in previous essays (essay nos. 5–9), who otherwise profoundly disagreed on many important issues, were one regarding the origins of the social contract. For all three, the social contract was founded on the consent of the people.

Hume (1711-1776) disagrees violently. The origins of the social contract, argues Hume, have been wrongly conferred on consent, the consent of the people. This is far from the truth, and is a misreading of recorded history. Hobbes and Locke, falsely presupposed that people who obeyed government were genuinely convinced that the Deity commanded us so, and worse, that people obeyed government out of a sense of lived obligation, and that the people thought it is both sacrilegious and unreasonable to disobey their rulers.

In direct contrast, he writes, "I shall venture to affirm, that both these systems of speculative principle are just; though not in the sense, intended by the parties; and that both the schemes of practical consequences are prudent;

though not in the extreme, to which each party, in opposition to the other, has commonly endeavored to carry them (*Of the Original Contract*, p. 276).

For Hume, "Almost all the governments, which exist at present, or of which there remains any record in story, have been founded originally, either on usurpation or conquest, or both, without any pretense of a fair consent, or voluntary subjection of the people" (p. 277).

Force, brute force, is the original cement of the social contract in any form of government. All that it takes to found a government is one bold man who surrounds himself by a strong army, and then willfully imposes himself on the people. This was Machiavelli's original insight, in *The Prince*, which Hume has made his very own.

The people are imposed upon, they never willingly consented, he adds emphatically. The bold ruler uses tyrannical methods to keep the people in check. The ruler divides his immediate subordinates, and terrorizes the masses. By the techniques of discipline and punish, and by the effective art of manipulation the social contract is preserved. Later historians and philosophers come to the scene to read fear as consent, and coercion as obedience.

Even the republic of Athens, reported to have been an extensive democracy was founded on the tombs of slavery and the subjection of women. Three-fourths of the population were slaves. Hume writes "that the establishment was not, at first, made, nor any law ever voted, by a tenth of those who were bound to pay obedience to it" (p. 278).

Unfortunately, when people obey government, it is not because they feel morally obligated. One wishes, as Locke does, that it is so. More often, they are compelled to obey by fear and necessity. Consent then is a figment of the philosopher's imagination.

Moral duties are of two kinds, suggests Hume. The first are those to which men are drawn by instinct, unencumbered by any rationality of interests. Examples are the love of children or pity for the unfortunate. Once humans discover instincts are good for society, we can use them to found society, glued by pity and love, if we can.

The second are entirely produced by fear and necessity. Examples are justice, fidelity or the observance of promises. These obligations can be forced on people. Rulers have exactly done that. They are not rational consequences of deliberation as Hobbes forcefully argued in the *Leviathan*, and as Locke added emphatically, in the *Two Treatises on Government*.

Hume is much closer to Rousseau, who like Hume tends to think that the authority of force is what compelled modern man to accept his miserable condition. Therefore, concludes Hume, moral obligation is a function of fear and necessity and not respects for the Deity, and most certainly not a consequence of deliberative reasoning from rational interests.

FROM

The Ethiopian Reporter, October 26, 2001.

SOURCE

David Hume, *Of the Original Contract*, Oxford University Press, USA, 1960.

13

JAMES MADISON AND THE FEDERALIST

The Federalist papers are models of brilliant journalistic theorizing on the structure and ends of government. They were a collection of newspaper articles written by three youthful writers, James Madison, Alexander Hamilton and John Jay. Their articles appeared regularly in *New York Press*, beginning October 27, 1787.

Of the three, Madison is the one who had the makings of a brilliant political theorist, well versed in classical theories of government, and who actually attempted in his articles to engage some perennial themes in philosophy. He chose to engage two such themes, human nature and the ends of government.

Humans are faction-forming beings, theorizes Madison, in his justly famous *Federalist 10*. By faction, Madison understands "A number of citizens, whether amounting to a majority or minority of the whole, who are united and actuated by some common impulse of passion, or of interest, adverse to rights of other citizens" (*Federalist 10*, p. 54).

Factions are like incurable diseases. Their effects can be controlled. Their causes are indeterminate, since they are essential parts of human nature, so they cannot be cured. There are some methods of removing their causes. One can destroy the liberty that creates faction; or one can give the same passions, interests and desires to all humans, so that they do not ever have to fight. Their passions can be equalized. To destroy liberty for the sake of removing faction is neither wise nor smart. To spread the same passions to all human beings is not practical.

The first goal of government is the protection of liberty, including the formation of faction. True, faction has been the cause of class warfare and deep inequalities among human beings for millennia. But that is no reason to remove faction.

The purpose of government, as Hobbes and Locke compellingly argue and with whom Madison agrees, is not the removal of faction, but the control of its effects. Government could do this through powerful legislation. Pure democracy, Karl Marx notwithstanding, cannot ever remove faction, but it can regulate its excesses.

Where pure democracy fails, Madison argues that a republic, following Emmanuel Kant, can succeed. A republic, unlike pure democracy, is guided by a modest conception of human possibilities.

First of all, one of the obvious sources of faction has been, and in this he agrees with Marx, about "unequal distribution or property. Those who hold and those who are without property have ever formed distinct interests in society. Those who are creditors, and those who are debtors, fall under a like discrimination" (p. 56).

These diverse interests must be regulated by an effective legislation. For Madison, regulating property, and not merely preserving it by the powers of the state, as Locke argues, is the chief end of government. Justice ought to balance liberty and the excesses of it, as Plato was the first to point out.

It is the duty of an enlightened leader, argues Madison, to legislate class differences in income, wealth and power, by the balance of justice.

FROM

The Ethiopian Reporter, September 3, 2001.

SOURCE

James Madison, *Federalist 10,* New York: Modern Library, 1937.

14

DEMOCRACY AS CHECKS AND BALANCES

The regulation of inequalities is a central task of a good government and now following Madison I will interpret the method of checks and balances as a way of systematically controlling the abuse of power by diffusing it into several chambers that will check on each other.

As we recall, Locke was the first to suggest the division of power into several branches. Madison takes that suggestion to heart, and uses it to develop the thesis that democracy is essentially a method of accommodating human nature. As he put it so eloquently, "If men were angels, no government would be necessary. If angels were to govern men, neither external nor internal controls on government would be necessary. In framing a government which is to be administered by men over men, the great difficulty lies in this: you must first enable the government to control the governed; in the next place oblige it to control itself" (*Federalist 10,* 51).

In a republican form of government power must be diffusely focused. There should not be one center of power, as in tyranny, but multiple sources. The ultimate source of power, of course, should be the people, whose power is localized in the legislature. The legislative branch should be further divided between the people and their elected representatives. The executive branch, on the other hand, should not be diffuseded but fortified. To argue that it should be fortified is not to suggest that it should not be checked. That is far from the truth. Indeed, the misuse of authority takes place in alarming ways in this site of power, which should at all times be checked by a vigilant and highly informed legislature. Madison hints at numerous ways of guarding the nation from the misuse of authority by a zealous and tyrannical sovereign.

In a federal republic both the federal government and the states should be guided by the maxim that power can be checked only by power, hence a system of checks and balances must be the guide. All the power delegated by the people to their representatives is concentrated in the federal government. Dividing power between the federal government and the states further controls any possible usurpation of power. The people's power is twice defended on two levels: division of power on the federal level, and defending state rights from federal usurpation. Throughout the system power is controlled by power.

Furthermore, it is crucial, given the nature of factions, that the majority faction does not dominate the minority. It is the cardinal duty of government to create a common good above the particular goods of factions. Civil rights and religious rights of the people must be articulated and defended by an impartial government.

Justice must be the goal of government, instructs Madison.

FROM

The Ethiopian Reporter, October 17, 2001.

15

IMMANUEL KANT ON REPUBLICANISM

Immanuel Kant lived between 1724 and 1804. What Kant had in mind by republicanism is totally different from our current understanding of the term. Nor did he equate it with democracy, and he emphatically distinguished it from despotic monarchy, including constitutional monarchy. Indeed, this form is Kant's own original construction.

Highly enlightened citizens inhabit his republican form as he idealized his regime. The enlightened citizen subjects of this regime are expected to fully disburden themselves from tutelage to self-imposed bondage to despotic and unenlightened leaders. These citizens are enlightened because they are resolutely determined to use their reason to legislate for themselves, to use reason and recognize incompetent and indecent leaders. Such citizens are environed by a philosophic atmosphere, and are accustomed to critical thinking, and to deciding for themselves. Impostors do not bamboozle them.

Following Hobbes, and sharply departing from Rousseau, whom he otherwise greatly admired, Kant argues that "The state of peace among men living side by side is not a natural state (status naturalis); the natural state is one of war. A state of peace, therefore, must be established" ("Perpetual Peace," Section ii, p. 92).

The establishment of such a republic guided by the utopian vision of perpetual peace is the task of practical reason; it is the function of philosophy's practical moral task. A republican form of government is the appropriate form suitable for the disposition of enlightened citizens. One way by which this political form can be realized is through the writing of a comprehensive constitution that guarantees "the principles of freedom of the members of society; secondly, by principles of dependence of all upon a single common legislation (as subjects); and thirdly, by the law of their equality (as citizens). The republican constitution, therefore, is, with respect to law, the one, which is the original basis of every form of civil constitution. The only question now is: Is it alone the one, which can lead to perpetual peace" (Section ii, p. 94).

Kant is quick to inform us that this political form should not be confounded with the democratic form. Whereas the democratic form could easily be despotic in the hands of the people, the despotic form controls the possibility of despotism by genuinely enlightening the citizenry. The political principles of republican constitution carefully separate the executive power from the legislative power. Although Locke is not mentioned, Kant is clearly following his footsteps, and attacking Rousseau for refusing to divide sovereignty into alienable chambers, as I reported in an essay on Rousseau (essay no. 9).

Kant realizes that this utopia of an enlightened republic is hard to establish in practice, and almost impossible to preserve once constructed, because humans are not angels, and their selfish inclinations stand in the way, as we learned from Hobbes and Madison.

However, this form can come into being through a practical constitution, or so the philosopher hopes. And hope is all that philosophy can offer. There are no guarantees. Kant knew that very well. Yet he argues that modern man's selfish inclinations could be rechanneled toward philosophy. Humans can be morally and politically reorganized. Man can be forced to "be a good citizen even if not a morally good person." The moral organization of man is a practical and political task. As Kant put it humorously, "The problem of organizing a state, however, hard it may seem, can be solved even for a race of devils, if only they are intelligent" (Section ii, p. 112).

A good constitution can mobilize this intelligence, in service of humanity, and produce a good moral condition of the citizens; whereas it would be ludicrous to think that morality can produce a good citizen by itself. Perhaps Rousseau idealizes man too much; to think that it is only modernity that we must blame for corrupting man. As we recall for Rousseau, natural man is morally organized whereas modern man is not. Kant sides with Hobbes against Rousseau on this point.

The smart legislator can work with man as if he is a devil and subtly reeducate him to be at least a good citizen. Man, argues Kant, is simultaneously attracted to sociability and solitude. Man is by nature antagonistic. This antagonism can produce a good thing. A state can be organized in such a way that it can minimize the danger of man's warring nature, if Hobbes and Kant are right, and maximize man's potential peacefulness, if Rousseau's vision of man makes sense.

FROM

The Ethiopian Reporter, November 1, 2001.

SOURCE

Immanuel Kant, "Perpetual Peace," *On History*, ed. Lewis White Beck, Macmillan/Library of Liberal Arts, 1963.

16

HEGEL ON THE STATE: AN INTRODUCTION

Hegel's revolutionary conception of the state has no precedent among the modern philosophers who preceded him. Neither Rousseau, to whom Hegel is the closest, nor Kant, against whom Hegel's dialectical method and revolutionary content is opposed root and branch, are his competitors. Among the moderns, Hegel and his dialectical method, right or wrong, is genuinely original. Couple his originality with the difficulty of his prose; you will see a lonely star shining in the sky.

So what does Hegel say about the state, the democratic state. He says very much that is stunning, and not always clearly. He has his moments of brilliant clarity and mesmerizing eloquence. But such moments are very rare. He is simply a difficult philosopher, but never a windbag. The student of Hegel is amply rewarded, if he withstands the stylistic torture. The experience is well worth the reward, however.

Hegel begins with the statement; "The state is the actuality of the ethical Idea." (*The Philosophy of Right*, para. 257).

Translating it to regular language, the state is the culmination of a long historical process that idealized the birth and maturity of states such as Plato's that sought to organize states in which the individual felt at home, lived as if he or she created the institutions. *The Republic* of Plato is one such long meditation that was hastily treated as a nonrealizable idea.

To Hegel's credit he took this ideal as a rational and practicable idea. States have always existed in custom and tradition. Individuals, however, rarely feel that they can be their own conscious constructions, provided that they are guided by a rational idea, which is then used to organize a state. The more aware the individual is about his role in realizing the rational idea, the more concrete and real the state is. Hegel is the first to make a conscious link between the individual and the institutions of the state. Previous to Hegel, with the exception of Plato and Rousseau, as we recall, the individual was not so empowered. Institutions were alien to his being. They felt less than created institutions and more like alien impositions.

The more the state embodies itself in the activities of the individual as a constructor of institutions, the more rational the state is. The quality and quantity of belonging that the individual experiences measure the rationality of the state to an existing state. A state that is external to the individual in the form of dead custom is not as rational as a state that is created by the mind and the will of the individual. In an obscure passage Hegel writes, "Rationality, taken generally and in the abstract, consists in the thorough going unity of the universal and the single. Rationality, concrete in the state, consists (a) ...in the unity of objective freedom and (b) ... in self-determining action on laws and principles which are thought and so universal" (par. 258).

States founded on custom, fear, trust or coercion, as David Hume pointed out, are not rational. Fear and freedom cannot be confused. Freedom is the basis for consciously rational freedom. Hegel more than Kant, who stressed the role of reason in the establishment or the republican form of government, is wedded to the defense of freedom, and to the birth of actual, and not merely ideal, states fashioned by the vision of freedom. Hegel credits Rousseau for this far-reaching articulation of freedom.

The state is the actuality of freedom argues Hegel. Freedom is actualized as a principle of freedom. In such a state, individuals are not only the bearers of rights, but also willing performers of actual duties because such citizens readily know that the state is nothing without their duties. For such citizens the state is a living institution that depends on their wills and obligations. The state is their internal life. They have internalized their duties as conscious citizens. The state is not an alien institution to them, since its institutions, such as the constitution, enshrined the principle of freedom, as their actual construction.

From

The Ethiopian Reporter, November 6, 2001.

Source

G.F. Hegel, *Philosophy of Right*, New York: Oxford University Press, 1952.

17

HEGEL ON THE ETHICAL STATE AND THE IDEA OF LAW

The idea of the state produces the principle of freedom, consciously enshrined in the democratic constitution, as the highest expression of the idea of freedom. A state that reaches this level of political maturity, argues G.F. Hegel, is precisely the state that has realized itself as rational. Rational also is the constitution that confidently extends freedom with responsibility to individual members of the state.

The degree and quality of the freedoms that the citizens are exercising determine the actual power of the state. I call this freedom, the natural property of democratic personalities. Such personalities live in freedom responsibly. They avoid excesses and deficiencies, precisely because they are politically mature, and have internalized moderation as a way of life, as we learned from Aristotle, as I argued in "Revisiting Classical Democracy" (essay no. 4).

The individual flourishes only under the condition of freedom. The rational state knows that and joyously extends this freedom to the person yearning for it. What we call freedom, teaches Hegel, is nothing more than the concrete realization of legitimately lived freedom. To be free is to concretely live in freedom.

Freedom is always concrete. It is lived legitimately. It is self-regulating. It respects the authority of the law. Those who live their lives this way demand rights from the rational state because they dutifully obey the laws of the constitution. Rights and duties interpenetrate this way. Rational citizens of the democratic state know this. As Hegel put it, "in the State duty and right are united in one and the same relations" (*Philosophy of Right*, par. 261).

Hegel adds perceptively, "Slaves have no duties, because they have no rights, and vice versa" (par. 261). Furthermore, the idea of the state has three moments, (a) constitutional law, (b) international law and (c) world history.

Concrete freedom is represented in personal individuality. The needs and desires of particular individuals realize their complete development and explicit recognition first in the family, second in civil society and third and maturely in the ethical and rational state.

In the state, all members of the state recognize rights and duties. Rights and duties become concrete universals. They command action by their universality. Unlike life in civil society, where there are no binding rules, other than a system of needs by atomistic monads, life in the state is ethical, needs to interpenetrate and responsibility is fully realized. Life in the ethical state elevates these needs from the strife of particularities to the status of binding universality. Everyday life is ethical. Competition is replaced by cooperation among mature individuals.

Duty in the state is experienced as an absolute need, produced by the rational individual. Rules are not coercive, but obligatory. Obligation is the natural property of citizenship. Rights are moments of duty. Duty and right are enshrined in the constitution as expressions of concrete freedom. We are back to where we began. Hegel reminds us, in a difficult passage, "The constitution is rational insofar the state inwardly differentiates and determines its activity in accordance with the nature of the concept. The result of this is that each of these powers is itself the totality of the constitution, because each contains the other moments, being expressions of the differentiation of the concept, simply abide in their ideality and constitute nothing but a single individual whole" (par. 2720).

Thus the division of power created by the law and promulgated in the constitution into the legislative and executive is nothing more than the rationalization of the law by rational individuals, in the form of thinkers as responsible and mature decision-makers. Enlightened monarchs and rational civil servants are chosen to perform their tasks because their charter and skills are guided by the idea of rationality.

FROM

The Ethiopian Reporter, September 26th, 2001.

SOURCE

G.F. Hegel, *Philosophy of Right,* New York: Oxford University Press, 1952.

18

MARX ON SOCIALIST DEMOCRACY

Karl Marx, was keenly interested in democracy. His life-long project was the articulation of an original political form, which I would like to call socialist democracy, SD for short. The best place to look for the appropriated ingredients out of which one can fashion SD are Marx's *Economic and Philosophical Manuscripts of 1844.*

For Marx, democracy in its bourgeois form must be abolished, through communism. Communism itself, Marx writes, "is the positive suppression of private property as human self-estrangement, and hence the true appropriation of the human essence through and for man; it is the complete restoration of man to himself as social, i.e. human being... this communism, as fully developed humanism equals natu-ralism...the entire movement of history is therefore both the actual act of creating communism" (*Early Writings*, p. 348).

The democracy that Marx yearned for, although not explicitly, can come into being only after the abolition of private property. The creation of classes and the capital that they command, the uneven spread of wealth and power, that capital creates, prevents the possibility of those unpropertied masses to run for offices so as to determine their fate. That is why for Marx—before we can talk about the division and delegation of power to the legislative, executive and judicial branches, which are the heart of liberal democracy—the pernicious influence of wealth and power must be ended.

This is a political argument, that in effect is asking for political struggle. The most moral faction of the propertied classes can easily design bourgeois democracy; socialist democracy can be effected only by the activity of the working class. This form cannot be handed in peacefully. It requires agency, political struggle by the powerless. Communism is an activity of political becoming and not, as Hegel thought, the becoming of the rational idea and the rational state that embodies that idea.

The humanization of man and the naturalization of man can take place after genuine democracy, the democracy of poor people is effected in the designing of institutions that would feed, shelter and clothe the needy, without qualifying them through private property.

As Marx put it, "Private property has made us so stupid and one sided that an object is ours only when we have it, when it exists for us as capital or when we directly possess, eat, drink, wear, inhabit it, etc., in short when we use it... therefore all the physical and intellectual senses have been replaced by the simple estrangement of all these senses—the sense of having." (p. 352)

These possessive senses must be replaced by sharing senses. Marx is calling for the reconstitution of man before one could talk about a suitable organization of the state. Once the possessive senses are abolished, the management of resources and the administration of humans can easily accommodate the highly efficient checks and balances implicit in Locke's division of power into the three branches.

Marx did not work out any political form. What he gave us is a rich vision of our possibilities, and he was convinced that the possessive senses are dehumanizing and denaturalizing man, and that they must be abolished. The political form—that is, the organization of the state—cannot be decided until after "having" is replaced with "being," competition is replaced with cooperation, and violence is replaced with discourse. The appropriate form of democracy for humans leads Marx in his political letters to address the larger question of the organization of the state, which is the subject of the next essay.

FROM

The Ethiopian Reporter, November 21, 2001.

SOURCE

Karl Marx, *Economic and Philosophical Manuscripts of 1844,* New York: Vintage, 1968.

19

MARX ON THE STATE AND PURE DEMOCRACY

The state is the organization that confers rights and liberties on its members, according to Hegel. The state as an ethical community does this with great authority, added Hegel. This is a poignant vision that Hegel introduced to political theory. Marx critiques this view and proceeds in the opposite direction. Whereas Hegel wanted to preserve the state as a superior organizational form to civil society, Marx wants to abolish the state, through a total social revolution, the activities of the workers themselves.

Marx writes, "The State will never discover the source of social evils in the State and the organization of society, as the Prussian expects of his King. Wherever there are political parties each party will attribute every defect of society to the fact that its rival is at the helm of State instead of itself. Even the radical and revolutionary politicians look for the causes of evil not in the nature of the State but in a specific form of the State which they would like to replace with another form of the State" (*Critical Notes on the King of Prussia and Social Reform*, p. 411).

Penetrating statements such as this have given the name anarchist to Marx. For Marx, however, the creation of stateless society can realize pure democracy. Marx, like Hegel, wants to abolish civil society; unlike Hegel, Marx wants to abolish the state, the political organ of the ruling class.

Poverty, pauperism, begging, stealing, the plight of the poor cannot be solved by the administration of a better state, Marx argues, with a bitter melody of injustice. They are gasping for total revolution. These human problems are deeper than political problems. As such they cannot be solved politically; they can be canvassed as human problems, calling for a redefinition of our humanity.

Administrative panacea is a chimera of a solution. A social revolution attentive to these deep inequalities is a total revolution. Such a totality requires the emancipation of the alienated human senses. These senses have impoverished man. Humans have to be disalienated from themselves, from work, from other human beings, from the products of their labor and from the human species. This disalienation is not the function of another state. It calls for the abolition of any state form, and the reinstallment of a genuine society, as a community, guided by a common good, defined by the proletariat.

Poverty and pauperism exist, argues Marx, only because the state exists to perpetuate them. This miserable human reality can be changed by effective critical/revolutionary activity. The social soul of revolution demands categorically the abolition of the state. The state form is simply unsuitable for the magnitude of the human problem. This social revolution must topple the old ruling class, which wants to maintain the state by any means necessary. The ruling class enjoys alienation. The poor hate it but do not know how to change it. The social revolution is the political act of the oppressed.

It is the social form of revolution. Through these arguments Marx provided a social theory of change and revolution.

For Marx, socialist democracy is the result of total social revolution. As Marx put it, "Without revolution Socialism cannot be made possible" (p. 420). Democracy for Marx meant the abolition of the private and the public, including the abolition of private property along with the state that naturalized the idea.

Finally, Marx argues, "The legislature is representative only in the sense that every function is representative. For example, the cobbler is my representative only insofar as he satisfies a social need…in this sense he is a representative not by virtue of another thing he represents by virtue of what he is and does" (*The Civil War in France*, pp. 189-90).

Politics in the end is nothing more the administration of things. The new form of the administration of resources replaces the old view of politics as the administration of people by society under the management of the people's representatives, chosen by the people themselves. This new paradigm does not require the state. The task could be performed by society. The administration of humans through the state gives way, for the first time in human history, to an intelligent management of things by society. The distinction between society and the state disappears. Humans become members of the community, in which being and sharing with others is more important than having things.

FROM

The Ethiopian Reporter, November 21, 2001.

SOURCES

Karl Marx, *The Civil War in France*, (International Publishers, New York, NY, 1989).

Karl Marx, *Critical Notes on the Article "The King of Prussia and Social Reform*,*"* Vorwärts, No. 63, Berlin, August 7, 1844.

20

ALEXIS DE TOCQUEVILLE: DEMOCRACY IN AMERICA

Alexis de Tocqueville, a French aristocrat, lived from 1805 to 1859. Tocqueville at the young age of 26 came to America to study the prison system. He ended up being an acute observer of American democratic institutions, which led to the writing of *Democracy in America*.

The democracy that he so sensitively dissected with a surgeon's precision is the democracy of checks and balances so ably designed by James Madison that is enshrined in the American Constitution and is now part and parcel of American political culture.

For Tocqueville, democracy, whatever else it entails, has attained a concrete political form, that I wish to call liberal democracy. In America, argues the French aristocrat, the people are the supreme governors of their institutions. It is the sovereign people who appoint their legislators, choose the executive and furnish the jurors.

Furthermore, in America, argues Tocqueville, the passion for equality has become a cardinal political principle. Every citizen has internalized equality. All Americans think and behave that they are the equal of everybody. Class barriers are salient. Democratic institutions have fostered and fortified this uncontrollable zeal for equality.

The advantages of democracy are many. Democratic principles propelled by the vast wind of equality promote the general welfare of the greatest number of citizens. Indeed, this value is the first principle of democracy. There are more.

The interests of the whole are paramount. Particular interests are secondary, unless they are intimately related to general interests. The interests of society ought to be in harmony with particular interests of leaders. If leaders are caught advancing their interests at the expense of society's they will not be voted in again. As he put it, "When the rich alone govern, the interest of the poor is always endangered... the advantage of democracy does not consist, therefore, as has sometimes been asserted, in favoring the prosperity of all, but in simply contributing to the well-being of the greatest number" (p. 132).

The government of democracy extends the notion of political right to the poorest segment of the population. This ideal, much admired by Tocqueville, is the second principle of democracy. Everyone, with the exception of slaves and servants, exercises their political rights.

American democracy, he discovered, is maintained by several forces. The first is the powerful federal form, and the way it has spread its tentacles to the body politic; the second are the townships and the way they control potential federal despotisms; the third is the power of the judiciary; the final and most important force is the supreme power of custom— the customs of the people.

The "habits of the heart" are incredibly effective sources of political obligation, mediated through religion. Catholicism, in particular, systematically socializes citizens to be faithful. In America, he observes, religion directs the customs of the community, and, by regulating domestic life, it regulates the state. Religion seeks to make the citizen just, therefore, fair and compassionate. Americans do not learn political obligation from books. They learn by practicing legislation.

American democracy, however, is profoundly endangered by the condition of the three races, as he calls them. According to custom Americans believe that whites are the most intelligent, morally and technically; below them are the blacks; below the blacks are the Indians. He writes, "These two unhappy races have nothing in common, neither birth, nor features; nor language, nor habits" (p. 201), and although the law may abolish slavery, God alone can obliterate the traces of its existence. Furthermore, he concludes, "Those who hope that the Europeans will ever be amalgamated with the Negroes appear to me to delude themselves" (p. 223).

FROM

The Ethiopian Reporter, December 5, 2001.

SOURCE

Alexis de Tocqueville, *Democracy in America*, New York: Vintage Book, 1945.

21

DEMOCRATIC VALUES

In the previous essay I reported following Tocqueville that liberal democracy has a tremendous passion for equality, which Americans have made a very integral part of an American personality. Nowadays Americans have a passion for liberty also. But equality and liberty do not always go hand in hand. Liberty fosters individualism. Too much liberty produces selfishness. Selfishness does not always respect the passion for equality.

Men living in democratic societies tend to develop too many passions. Therefore, it is not surprising that Americans display as many passions as they do, argues Tocqueville. Most of these tend to be passion for wealth, for powers. So he argues, he had never been to a society of such restless entrepreneurs driven by desire and ambition, to move out of their original modest position to a higher one. Nowadays all Americans struggle to acquire property, if they have none, and would seek to accumulate where they are modestly propertied. One car produces the desire to have a second one. One is never enough. Two is adequate. More is better and securer.

Desire multiplies numbers; liberty justifies them. As he put it, "A native of the United States clings to this world's goods as if he were certain never to die; and he is so hasty in grasping all within his reach that one would suppose he was constantly afraid of not living long enough to enjoy them. He clutches everything, he holds nothing fast, but soon loosens his grasp to pursue fresh gratifications" (*Democracy in America*, p. 431).

Hence an American plans everything early on. Life insurance, in case he dies; the remaining can benefit. He builds or buys a house for his old age. He must have a summer house by the water; a winter house in the mountains; a studio in the city. He will travel miles to quiet his restless nerves, yearning for constant gratification.

Democratic desire and the promise of equality provoke all this restlessness. Nondemocratic nations cannot afford these values. Capital accumulation and the wonders of wealth and prosperity premise these values.

Only in democratic nations is the equality of conditions realized. The ideal of equality, the sheer dream that anything is realizable and obtainable by hard and honest work, propels so many of the best, the youngest and the most energetic to follow the paths of desire. They may or may not get there, but the mere fact that they are free to go anywhere moves so many souls, energizes so many bodies and feeds so many desires.

The ideal of equality is the intoxicant, liberty is the stimulant. Liberal democracy consciously elevated the passions of liberty and equality that many are encouraged to pursue, although few seem to get chosen. It is the merit of Tocqueville to have successfully exposed the pillars of liberal democracy, democracy at work.

FROM

The Ethiopian Reporter, December 5, 2001.

SOURCE

Alexis de Tocqueville, *Democracy in America*, Volume II, Vintage Books 1959.

22

John Rawls and Contemporary Liberal Democracy

John Rawls, a leading contemporary American philosopher, is the voice of liberal democracy. He considers himself as an appropriator and original interpreter of the democratic vision first enunciated by the social contract philosophers, Jean Jacques Rousseau, Thomas Hobbes and John Locke, whose views I interpreted in my previous essays (essay nos. 5–9). Rawls' intention, he tells us, is to answer certain fundamental questions concerning the philosophical foundation of liberalism in general and democratic liberalism in particular.

The first question is what is the most appropriate conception of justice that specifies fair terms of cooperation among free and equal human beings?

The second question is what are the grounds of toleration among diverse human beings, divided by different religious, philosophical and moral beliefs?

The final question is how does one sustain a form of liberal democratic society across generations once it is carefully constructed?

Answering the first question requires the development of two principles of justice, which can be used in the designing of the basic structure of society, that is the social, political and economic institutions of a democratic society suitably constructed.

The two principles are:

1. Each person has an equal claim to a fully adequate scheme of equal basic rights and liberties, which scheme is compatible with the same scheme for all; and in this scheme the equal political liberties, and only those liberties, are to be guaranteed their fair value.

2. Social and economic inequalities are to satisfy two conditions: first, they are to be attached to positions and offices to all under conditions of fair equality of opportunity; and second, they are to be to the greatest of the least advantaged members of society (*Political Liberalism*, p. 6).

A democratic society cannot afford, lest it seeks to destroy itself, to design institutions to squander the limited resources of citizens without a systematic plan guided by principles of justice. The citizens' money, intelligence, imagination and moral sense must be used in the shaping of the basic structure. Policy makers should not plan in the dark. Political ideals must guide public discourse. The public reason of the citizens must be consulted, argues Rawls.

All that citizens have to do in order to enter this moral zone, is use their reasoning power, which includes the moral sense of cooperation along with their rationality, which articulate their unique life plans, in the construction of rules and procedures, when they deliberate about the content of principles of justice for the basic structure. There is no coercion as in totalitarian regimes but plenty of discourse and debate through the engagement of public reason, the reason of citizens.

By appealing to our reasoning ability we can curb our greed and selfishness for the sake of the whole. In this way cooperation becomes habitual, and eventually a moral way of life, a grammar of living. Doing this does not require a moral gene. It is an act of reason and rationality.

If we like what Rawls is proposing, we can realize it by wearing a veil of ignorance and by placing ourselves in an "original position." This is a place from which we can legislate for human beings without being encumbered by race, gender, sex, class position and moral structure. All that we need is our reasoning power and our rational endowment to articulate the most just way of designing a society that would benefit us all, for generations to come. In a nutshell this is Rawls' vision of a well-ordered society.

FROM

The Ethiopian Reporter, December 26, 2001.

SOURCE

John Rawls, *Political Liberalism*, New York: Columbia University Press, 1993.

23

PARTICIPATORY DEMOCRACY

Ethiopia is in dire need of democracy—a particular kind of democracy it has never had in its long history. Its industrious and spiritual people need it. The leaders continue to deny it to us. Ordinary intellectuals and we Ethiopians would like to participate. We know what we must do. Our leaders do not trust us. They do not think that we are capable and willing.

The modalities of democracy that I have been surveying in these essays do not stress participation, with the exception of Rousseau and Marx. The rest are all the proponents of representative democracy.

I would like to defend participatory democracy on the local level, with a system of checks and balances on a national level. Unlike the advocates of representative democracy who separate representation from participation as moments of democracy, for me democracy is essentially participatory, and that participation and democracy are inseparable moments of democracy as a way of life.

Enabling people to participate in decisions that affect their ways of life implies that individuals are sufficiently intelligent to choose for themselves responsibly, and are willing and capable to assume responsibility and accountability for the choices they make. Fundamental political virtues such as responsibility, obligation, duty and accountability cannot be taught in the abstract through definitions and lectures. They must be practiced after we come of age. We become responsible, by acting responsibly; we feel obligated when we do things that obligation demands; we learn accountability by doing things and being accountable for them. When we are constantly responsible, accountable and obligable, the virtues insinuate themselves into our lives. They become habits of the heart. We do them joyously.

We Ethiopians ought to be given concrete opportunities to habitually practice these virtues of participatory democracy. We must practice these virtues at the workplace with our peers; at social occasions with our friends and relatives. Whenever we can we must habitually be responsible, accountable and obligable, without coercion by our leaders.

On the local level we must establish participatory institutions to run our affairs as citizens. We can establish groups at districts, municipalities, workplaces, hospitals and most important universities and schools to discuss issues before they are adopted as policies nationally.

So participation on the local level should be the practice among a manageable population. That is where issues should be exhaustively discussed. At the national level, through an intricate system of checks and balances, power could be divided among those who execute and judge, the executive and judiciary chambers, to enforce decisions and judge cases reached at the local legislative chamber of the people. The locus of power is the local level, where the people are directly participating in decisions that affect their lives, the production of commodities, and deciding what they necessarily need.

When leaders at the national level are found incompetent, they should be recalled, and be replaced by fresh voices. Democracy is always experimental. It is learned only through trial and error. People must be given a chance to lead and obey.

Reconciling the spirit of democracy's moments of participation and representation can be tried along the line which I am proposing here. These are complicated issues that I invite the public to deliberate on. The issues affect our lives, and our country is in dire trouble because we have not learned yet how to govern ourselves. We have tried many kinds of regimes, all the way from monarchy to authoritarian socialism. They have all failed.

The question now is what we should we try? How should we govern ourselves? I am suggesting in this essay that Ethiopia needs a radical democracy watered by the generosity of participation and by organized devices of checks and balances of power, the Madisonian political wisdom.

FROM

The Ethiopian Reporter, April 4, 2002.

24

PASSION FOR JUSTICE AND FREEDOM

Radical democracy, I wish to argue, needs some organizing principles. Justice and freedom are the most valuable principles of justice that a radically democratic regime needs, as I indicated in the previous essay. I should now wish to elaborate on it.

In Ethiopia, where these values are desperately lacking, it makes intuitive sense and is also extremely reasonable to suggest in the strongest sense possible that our leaders should draw both from the public reason of Ethiopian culture, and from their own selves, the creation and systematic diffusion of freedom and justice as powerful organizing tools of redesigning the basic structure in modern Ethiopia.

The existing Ethiopian state seems to be unable of distinguishing essential citizen needs from inessential habits of the elite. These two sets of desire need to be weighed by the balance of justice. Just because the rich and powerful can afford to have anything they wish, including those at the helm of power, it does not follow that that is both reasonable and rational.

It is a fact that the rich are rich because they made themselves rich, and think that they can stay rich. Reason, however, demands that sometimes the rich do become richer, by exploiting the poor. The Ethiopian state, however, cannot remain blind to this fact. I understand that, during the time of globalization, if the Ethiopian state is to remain afloat, it must accumulate capital by creating capitalists. Fine. The question is what kind of capitalists? The kinds who actually create capital and jobs are different from the capitalists who create capital, to waste it on consumption. To a great extent, Ethiopian capitalists at the moment seem to be conspicuous consumers, and not productive capitalists.

To argue this way is not to deny that the capitalist market is not important. Even ideas have to be marketed as are food products and health goods. In fact, I advise our leaders to invest in the education of compassionate but economically shrewd economists. This is a necessity without which Ethiopia cannot come out of the vicious cycle of poverty and famines.

The importance of knowing the cycles of the market, however, is different from the cultivation of experts with a moral vision. This point may seem obvious, but only in the area of saying it. Had it been too obvious the world market would be flooding with a flurry of compassion and care. It seems to be obvious only because we can say that even an urchin knows that compassion is good, but he does not know how to be compassionate. The same is true about those who think that creating a market with a human face is easy. Because they know that it is not, but they convince themselves to believe that it is.

I think on the other hand that it is much easier to neglect freedom and equality than it is to grant people the right to choose the life they would like to live, and not to treat them as equals but as inferiors, who are not entitled to anything. The passion for freedom and justice, however, is a natural property that we yet have to uncover.

From my own observation of family practices, I have come to realize that there is a practice of sharing whatever you have with those who do not. These practices constitute tradition. My parents have observed that silent rule. I am sure they are not the only ones. Over centuries of Ethiopian civic life, and against the background of frequent famines and hardships, Ethiopians have developed a culture of shared destinies. We Ethiopians have been humbled not to judge the poor of deserving their condition. Our Christianity has taught us to empathize with the poor and the meek. These are precious values.

The freedom and equality that I am arguing to function as the organizing principles of a radically democratic Ethiopian regime is already a well-woven fabric of tradition and customs. To a significant extent then it is a matter of extracting and uncovering it from tradition, and then generalizing the values to a level of national culture. Legislators and policy makers are to be able to distill these values from Ethiopian value systems themselves.

It is only recently that the Ethiopian state found itself surrounded by cutthroats and callous oligarchs whose gods are money and honor. Consequently, the respect for the value of the individual and the equality she deserves has been smeared with dirty money and vacuous honor. This has to change.

The bewildering phenomena of corruption and greed and new facets of rude Ethiopian capitalism must give way to a culture of sharing and modesty. This new culture must be spearheaded by a new breed of radical democrats, who must find an alternative to callous capitalism, without resorting to vulgar and totalitarian capitalism that does not understand the meaning of freedom.

FROM

The Ethiopian Reporter, March 3, 2004.

25

RADICAL DEMOCRACY: VISION AND MORALITY

The previous essays were devoted to an interpretation of democracy. The next few essays will focus on theorizing a modality of democracy that draws on Ethiopian culture, customs and historical values, and is effectively appropriate for Ethiopia. The interpretation of democracy of the previous essays was not premised on the assumption that Ethiopians should blindly imitate the versions of democracy articulated by a long list of Western philosophers, who rightly wrote from within the background of the particularity of the customs and traditions of their homelands. That was not my intention at all.

To even think this way for a moment is to subject Ethiopians, founders of a world civilization, to slavishness through imitation. There is much in our very own Ethiopian tradition that is worth preserving; there is also equally much that is not worthy of us, and which needs to be erased. Knowing what to erase and preserve is the challenge for an interpreter of Ethiopian history.

I will designate the version that is appropriate for Ethiopia: radical democracy. By radical I mean a return to an original root. By radical democracy, I understand a vision of human possibilities rooted in the language of the human heart, the home of moral intelligence, that stirs one to radical action on behalf of the negatively disadvantaged human beings, whose lives are marred by poverty, diseases and hopelessness.

My most recent visit in Ethiopia was marred by sadness mixed with joy. Sadness because of the plight of the poor, which has frozen in time; joy because I love my homeland and I adore to be surrounded by Ethiopians, from all walks of life.

A radical democrat is one who thinks with ordinary Ethiopians and for them. A radical democratic regime is organized by the principle of care and compassion for its citizens. The human heart, I will argue, is a composite of reason and moral sense. When the heart is consulted, it can summon the inner voice of reason to radical moral/political action. When the heart is thus consulted it imposes its laws on the will, provoking it to act, stirred by a self-imposed duty, and guided by imagination and intelligence.

The suitably consulted heart then precipitates with the right guidelines to the yearning left, who would otherwise dangle in indecision and doubt. The heart responds to our devoted consulting with concrete principles of moral and political action. The individual cannot any longer say she is helpless, she does know what to do. The encounter with the language of the heart, and the possibility of a summoning, demand from the self that it frees itself from engagement with the affairs of the world. The self has to ready itself for the deep encounter. Silence and quiet are the appropriate moods in which the self has to be, in order to prepare itself for a conversation with the inner voice of reason.

The summoning cannot occur amid the hustle and bustle of life. We cannot summon when we are bombarded with career plans, a house to buy, a promotion to get, making quick money, cocktail parties to attend and the restlessness of travel. All these obstruct the paths of the summons. They invade our horizons. Although they are ultimately meaningless, we invest them with meanings, with which we burden time. We do this so that we can say, I have no time.

Of course, that is an excuse, and we know it too. But we lie to ourselves. Worse still we blame time. But time has no agency. Time is in our hands. What is not in our hands is only death. Death is a master of time. We must make time. We have to learn to make time. Time does make itself. Time is an abstraction. It is us that give tasks in time and to time.

True humans are equal and free, as Rawls pointed out in essay no. 22. However they are also physically different, a point that Rousseau made, and which Rawls is appropriating suitably. We come to this world with different endowments and skills. Some of us are tall, others are short, a great number are in-between. Some of us enjoy counting grass, others excel in math, a few are born athletes and musicians.

These are simple natural and social facts. Some of these endowments unfortunately help some of us to be rich. Others are left behind the social lottery. Natural facts in this sense produce advantageous social reality for some individuals, and disadvantages are heaped on others. Only a well-ordered society can change reality when it brings misery to some human beings. Social theorists like Marx would attribute these disadvantages to the role of capital and the power of ideology. Rawls attributes some of the differences to nature.

The second democratic principle of justice suggests that these economic, social and political differences—in any society, capitalist or socialist—are bound to stay. No principle of justice, no matter how fair, can remove them. Like faction, as we learned from James Madison, these natural differences, caused by reason that we do not know, cannot be removed. But we can control the effects; namely, the alarming disparity in income and wealth can be effectively reordered by some practical principles of justice.

If we follow the directives of the second principle of justice that admonishes us not to pamper the well to do and neglect the poor, we would not be able to tolerate a society that allows executives to command huge salaries, when a single mother with four children works at two or more full-time dead-end jobs to make ends meet. Such a society Rawls would argue, is disordered. Ask yourself, is this fair? Is this reasonable? The answer to both questions is no.

If you as a citizen internalized something like the second principle, you can answer no as well. One does not have to be a genius to know how to rectify this unfair situation. It is simple. Reduce the salary of the CEO to a reasonable level, and increase the salary of the single mother correspondingly; or, if you can maintain the salary of the CEO, then increase the salary of the single mother modestly, relative to her expenses, her life plans and her dreams for her children. This kind of arrangement is both reasonable and rational.

Justice as fairness attempts to extend rights and liberties to those who have none. Given the fact that human beings are essentially equal—with some insignificant differences among them—all humans as free and equal are entitled to freely express their views, and have access to modest food, shelter, clothing and health, necessary for a complete morally civilized life. By the yardsticks of the first principle of justice, institutions, which deny liberties and rights to any citizen, are committing violence against the victims of poverty and ill health. They are shattering bodies and depressing souls, the bodies and souls of the poor. Humans who are denied the internal needs of the body are socially dead. These abstract principles could solve numerous social problems if the ruling party in modern Ethiopia adopts them.

FROM

The Ethiopian Reporter, January 10, 2004.

INDEX